4.00

e

THE RANGERS

Also by Brian McFarlane

It Happened in Hockey

More It Happened in Hockey

Still More It Happened in Hockey

The Best of It Happened in Hockey

Stanley Cup Fever

Proud Past, Bright Future

It Happened in Baseball

The Leafs

The Habs

THE RANGERS

BRIAN
MCFARLANE'S
ORIGINAL
SIX

BRIAN MCFARLANE

Stoddart

Published in 1997 by Stoddart Publishing Co. Limited
34 Lesmill Road, Toronto, Canada M3B 2T6

Distributed in Canada by General Distribution Services Inc.
34 Lesmill Road, Toronto, Canada M3B 2T6
Tel. (416) 445-3333 Fax (416) 445-5967
Email Customer.Service@ccmailgw.genpub.com

Distributed in the U.S. by General Distribution Services Inc.
85 River Rock Drive, Suite 202, Buffalo, New York 14207
Toll-free tel. 1-800-805-1083 Toll-free fax 1-800-481-6207
Email gdsinc@genpub.com

01 00 99 98 97 1 2 3 4 5

Cataloging in Publication Data

McFarlane, Brian, 1931–
The Rangers

(Brian McFarlane's original six)

ISBN 0-7737-3047-8

1. New York Rangers (Hockey team) – History – Anecdotes.
I. Title   II. Series: McFarlane, Brian, 1931–   .
Brian McFarlane's original six.

GV848.N43M33 1997   796.962'64'097471   97-931382-1

Cover design: Bill Douglas @ The Bang
Cover photo: Hockey Hall of Fame
Design and typesetting: Kinetics Design & Illustration

Printed and bound in Canada

To the Patricks, Emile Francis,
and Neil Smith, in appreciation of
their management skills

Contents

1

The Lester Patrick Years

The Frank Boucher Era

The Muzz Patrick Era

4

The Emile Francis Era

5

The Ferguson, Shero, Patrick, and Esposito Era

6

The Neil Smith Era

1

THE LESTER PATRICK
YEARS

Opening Night

O N November 16, 1926, the New York Rangers made their Madison Square Garden debut against the swashbuckling Montreal Maroons, a big, bruising club and the defending Stanley Cup champions. Lester Patrick's hastily assembled team, initially called Tex's Rangers, was the underdog. Someone had designed a crest for the Ranger jersey — a depiction of a cowboy on a bucking bronco with the rider holding a hockey stick aloft. But the cowboy and his mount were sent out to pasture when owner Tex Rickard rejected the artwork. They were replaced by the word Rangers splashed in diagonal letters across the front of the royal blue jersey.

Jimmy Walker, New York's popular mayor, accepted an invitation to drop the puck for the ceremonial faceoff in the opening game against the Maroons. But the mayor was still en route to Madison Square Garden when the big moment arrived. Fortunately, there was a stand-in.

Lois Moran, a beautiful movie star, was introduced to the crowd that filled the Garden. Most of the gentlemen fans, accustomed to Broadway openings, were attired in tuxedos. The ladies wore fashionable evening gowns, their jewelry sparkled under the overhead lights, and the applause was generous as Miss Moran, a former stripper at Minsky's Burlesque, minced across the ice, waving to her fans with one hand and holding a puck in the other. She dropped the disc carefully between the sticks of Nels Stewart, the hardrock center of the Maroons and spindly Frank Boucher, who was about to begin a Ranger playing and coaching career that would last for the next 29 years. He was one of only four Rangers on the ice who had played professionally. All the others were first-year pros.

Referee Lou Marsh, a full-time Toronto sportswriter, swooped in to retrieve the ceremonial faceoff puck, waited for Miss Moran to depart, then dropped the puck a second time. The game was underway and the Rangers were officially part of the NHL. New York quickly went offside and the clang of the referee's school bell, signaling the infraction, caused the fans to roar with laughter. "Look, he's using a cowbell!" someone shouted. "That's a riot."

Boucher would later state the opening game was "as rough as any ever played." Blood poured from cuts when high sticks connected, and the grunts from players bodied into the ice or boards could be heard 10 rows up. Marsh couldn't possibly see all the fouls — crosschecking, slashing, hooking, and holding. Even mild-mannered Frank Boucher, who accumulated only 119 penalty minutes in his entire career, got into it. When challenged by Montreal tough guy Bill Phillips, Boucher threw off his gloves and laced into his opponent. Phillips knocked him flat with a punch. Boucher bounced up and knocked Phillips to the ice. They each drew five-minute penalties. It was one of only three major penalties Boucher would receive in 14 seasons of pro hockey.

There was only one goal scored and it came late in the second period. The Cooks teamed up to beat Maroons' goalie Clint Benedict, who, years later, would introduce the first face mask to the NHL. Bill Cook flipped the puck over Benedict who struck the goalpost with his head in attempting the save. There was a lengthy delay while the semiconscious netminder received some medical attention before propping himself back in the net.

The Garden ice, soft to begin with, was in terrible condition by the third period. There was no Zamboni in those days, no resurfacing of the ice between periods. Workmen simply used heavy scrapers to remove the snow and slush that accumulated.

The Rangers withstood every Maroon attack and emerged from the contest bruised, battered, and most important, triumphant. They received a prolonged ovation at the end, the applause from the vast audience lingering long after the players were back in their dressing room, where they pounded each other on the back, as thrilled as the spectators were with the outcome.

"We beat the world champions," someone shouted.

"Did you hear that crowd?" a player shrieked. "They love us here."

Lester Patrick shook hands all around. "Boys, you play some more games like that and this franchise will be a huge success here in New York. It's really exciting to think of what's ahead for all of us. This is just the beginning."

The Early Rangers

T HE Rangers were a near unanimous choice to finish last in the American Division of the ten-team NHL. They had been a sorry-looking club in their training camp scrimmages held in Toronto, and Conn Smythe, a newcomer to pro hockey, bore the brunt of the blame for their apparent ineptness. Smythe had been hired to assemble a competitive team, and he got off to a fine start when he signed the Cooks and Boucher, former stars in the defunct Western Hockey League. From Minnesota, he brought in two strong defensemen, Ivan "Ching" Johnston and Clarence "Taffy" Abel (the first American-born player to become a regular in the NHL). Both were balding belters who could heave opponents over the boards or lay them out on the ice. He added goaltenders Lorne Chabot and Hal Winkler (who drew the opening game assignment even though Chabot would soon prove himself to be the better goaltender), Murray Murdoch (who played for the next 11 seasons without missing a game), smooth-skating Paul Thompson, Billy Boyd, Reg Mackey, and Oliver Reinikka.

When hockey people were asked what they thought of Smythe's player selections, they replied, "Not much." These words so unnerved Ranger president John Hammond that he fired Smythe during training camp and replaced him with Lester Patrick, a more experienced coach and manager. The articulate Patrick, then 42, would guide the Rangers from behind their bench for the next 13 years. When the NHL introduced All-Star voting in 1930–31, Patrick would be voted top coach in seven of the first eight seasons.

Another factor that led to Smythe's demise was a stubborn streak that infuriated Hammond. High-scoring "Babe" Dye was available to the Rangers, and Hammond was told that Dye would be a superstar if he played with the club.

"Sign him to a contract," he ordered Smythe.

"I will not," barked Smythe. "Dye's a goal scorer but he's not a good team man. I know him well and I won't have any part of him."

"I've heard that Dye's a great player and we should get him," Hammond insisted.

"You heard wrong," snorted Smythe.

Hammond sighed. "Connie," he said, "maybe you're too young and inexperienced for this job. Lester Patrick would jump at a chance to come to New York."

"Then hire Patrick," said Smythe, fire in his eye. "I've put a good team together for you and there's no room on it for "Babe" Dye. And if you hire Patrick, just make sure you pay me the money I'm owed."

Hammond promptly paid Smythe off and hired Patrick. As for "Babe" Dye, he never became a Ranger. He enjoyed a good season with Chicago, then went into a slump that netted him one goal in the next three seasons.

The Silver Fox:
A Hockey Legend

LESTER Patrick, the Silver Fox of hockey, reached the pinnacle in every phase of hockey — as a player, coach, manager, and owner. He would have refereed if they'd asked him — and no doubt excelled. One night in 1928, at age 44, he made history by donning the goal pads for a playoff game — and of course, winning it in overtime.

Lester was born December 30, 1883, in Drummondville, Quebec, the first of five sons sired by Joseph Patrick, a storekeeper and lumberman. At age nine, he sawed off the limb of a tree and made himself a hockey stick — one good enough for shinny. He received his first pair of skates when he was 10, and three years later, by now living in Montreal, he became a stick boy for the fabled Ottawa Silver Seven whenever they played games in Montreal.

He aspired to be a cowboy for a time, and gave it a try one summer after his freshman year at McGill University. But his true love was hockey. "I thought if I could play just one game in big-time hockey — I could die happy," he once told reporters. Tall, rawboned, and powerful, with a mop of hair that would turn silver prematurely and earn him his nickname, he broke into professional hockey in 1903 as a defenseman with the Brandon team in Manitoba. A part-time job in a laundry was part of the deal. In his first season, he wound up in a playoff series for the Stanley Cup, performing against the team he'd once guarded sticks for — the Silver Seven of Ottawa. During a long and fascinating career, he starred on defense with several teams and played on or managed 15 teams in Stanley Cup competition.

At age 22, Lester was captain of the famed Montreal Wanderers and led his team to three Stanley Cup triumphs. Then he traveled west to work with his father in the lumber business in Nelson, British Columbia. After work, he continued to play hockey in a semipro league.

A financial proposal he couldn't refuse brought him back east. He had offered his services to Art Ross's Montreal club for $1,200 and Ross had expressed horror at Patrick's demands. "No player is worth that kind of dough," snorted Ross, "except possibly myself." Ottawa and the little town of Renfrew, Ontario, also wanted Patrick. He told Ottawa he'd consider $1,500 and wired Renfrew that $3,000 was his price. "Renfrew's just a dot on the map," he told his brother Frank. "They'll never cough up $3,000, which is fine with me because I don't think I want to play there, anyway."

To his amazement, Lester received a wire back from Renfrew: "Proceed here at once. Will pay you $3,000." Still uncertain about a move to Renfrew, he sent another wire: "I'll report if you'll sign my brother Frank — at $2,000." Renfrew replied immediately: "Bring your brother. It's a deal."

Renfrew imported other top stars, and even offered Hay Millar, an Edmonton player, a thousand dollars to play a single game one time when Frank Patrick was injured.

The Patrick brothers were pioneers, among the first to realize that hockey was more than a winter pastime. It was big business.

It was in the summer of 1911 that the Patricks decided to introduce professional hockey to the Pacific coast. On his honeymoon that year in the east, Patrick investigated artificial ice rinks along the eastern seaboard in the United States. He returned to the Pacific coast, and with the backing of his wealthy father, and in partnership with brother Frank, built Canada's first artificial ice rinks in Vancouver and Victoria, British Columbia.

The Patricks launched the Pacific Coast Hockey League, a circuit that lasted for 15 years. They raided eastern teams for talented players and revolutionized the game with their innovations. They brought in the blue lines and the forward pass that made the game lightning fast. They added numbers to players' uniforms — a first in team sports. They devised the playoff system now in universal use in hockey and other sports.

In 1925, Lester Patrick's Victoria Cougars stunned the

Montreal Canadiens and won the Stanley Cup largely because he tried something new — using two forward lines. Until then, most players were 60-minute men.

In the summer of 1926, the Patricks sold all the players from the Coast League to the NHL. Weeks later, Lester signed with an NHL expansion team — the New York Rangers, replacing Conn Smythe, a young manager from Toronto who was fired before the opening game.

"That was embarrassing," Patrick once said. "I did know Connie Smythe. Then I had to go to Toronto where the Rangers were training and take over his job. In spite of this, Smythe was always one of my biggest boosters."

Patrick inherited a number of tough and talented players from Smythe, men like Taffy Abel, Ching Johnston, and the Cook brothers. As a result, the Rangers, in their initial season, captured first place in their division. Ranger star Bill Cook scored 33 goals in 44 games and won the scoring title. Patrick himself suited up for one game to display his defensive skills, and the following spring, he made another, much more stunning one-game comeback — as a goaltender — to help his Rangers win their first Stanley Cup.

With the Rangers, he devised plays and passing patterns that made the modern game a thing of beauty. It started with his number one line — the Cook brothers and Frank Boucher — and reached its ultimate in finesse and combination play with the Colville brothers and Alex Shibicky.

Shibicky once said, "Lester was more than a hockey great. He was a man who lived by a high moral code. He had a tremendous amount of personal feeling towards his players. He was an educated man in a tough sport. He would conduct classes in the Ranger dressing room, asking the capital city of nations and the names of rivers."

Patrick was brilliant and charming and had a gift for language. He was renowned as a raconteur. His best tales were told with a French Canadian dialect which he had acquired in his youth in Drummondville, Quebec. He was not without warts. He could be arrogant and short-tempered. Frank Boucher once said of him, "Lester could, in turn, be pleasant, excitable, kind, sarcastic, pompous, headstrong, understanding, gentle, callous, and contrite, depending on the circumstances."

Many of his rivals resented the adulation Patrick received from the New York media. They conceded that Lester had made huge contributions to the game of hockey, but they felt that Lester had convinced the New York writers that he had *invented* the game.

He coached the Rangers for 13 seasons and was named the NHL's outstanding coach in seven of eight years when the NHL began selecting All-Star teams in 1930–31.

On February 22, 1946, Patrick resigned as general manager of the Rangers. He was succeeded by the popular Boucher, an original Ranger, marking the beginning of the end of the friendship between the two men. Patrick agreed to stay on with the team in an advisory capacity, but during Boucher's first training camp in Winnipeg, Patrick complained loudly that Boucher neither sought nor wanted his advice. They seldom spoke to each other after that.

Patrick retired to Victoria where he ran a minor league hockey team. In his seventies, he fought his final battle — against cancer. The Silver Fox succumbed to the disease on June 1, 1960, at age 76.

Tributes poured in from all over North America. Perhaps old-time hockey great Newsy Lalonde said it best, "Whenever I look back on my career I always think of Lester, because he represented to me all the finest things about the game. He was a tremendous skater and stickhandler, he always played hard — a real never-say-die type — and he was a fine gentleman on and off the ice."

Chabot Shunned by Hockey Hall of Fame

GOALIE Lorne Chabot was a big man (six foot one and 185 pounds) in an era when most professional netminders were comparatively small. He joined the Rangers for their initial NHL season (1926–27) after leading his amateur team, Port Arthur, to back-to-back Canadian senior championships. He went on to play in 411 NHL games over 11 seasons with the Rangers and five other NHL clubs, compiling a sparkling goals-against average of 2.04 and an impressive total of 73 shutouts (eighth among all-time shutout leaders).

Chabot is remembered as the central figure in three of hockey's most historic games. As a Ranger, the goalie was cut over the eye by a rising shot in the 1928 playoffs against the Montreal Maroons and forced to retire. New York manager Lester Patrick, then 44, replaced Chabot in goal, helped win the game in overtime, and created one of hockey's best-loved "Believe It or Not" yarns.

In 1933, Chabot, by then a Toronto Maple Leaf, was in goal when the Leafs' little Ken Doraty won a playoff game over Boston at 4:46 of the sixth overtime period — the longest game played to that time. Three years later, playing for the Maroons, Chabot was the victim of a goal scored by Detroit's Mud Bruneteau that ended an even longer overtime. Mud's marker came at 16:30 of the sixth overtime period.

Chabot — known as "Old Bulwarks" — also saw service with the New York Americans, making him the most-traveled goalie of his era. The hotheaded netminder's mercurial temperament (he once punched a goal judge) was possibly responsible for his many uniform changes.

Still, there seemed to be no valid reason for the Rangers to dispose of him after his first two seasons in New York, during which he recorded 21 shutouts and goals-against averages of 1.56 and 1.79. He was even stingier in the playoffs (1.50 and 1.33) and added two more shutouts.

Lester Patrick, it's been said, wanted to move him because of the head cut he received in the 1928 playoffs. Patrick thought the injury would make him puck-shy. He traded Chabot to Conn Smythe's Leafs for Butch Keeling and goalie John Ross Roach, then watched in stony silence when Chabot and the Leafs trounced his Rangers in the Stanley Cup finals of 1932.

Chabot's stay in Manhattan required him to maintain a sense of humor. On his arrival in New York, two zany publicists took him aside and told him they were changing his name to Lorne Chabotsky.

"But why?" asked Chabot.

"Because a Jewish name will attract a lot of new fans to hockey," he was told.

Chabot shrugged and became Chabotsky overnight. The nom de plume disappeared after a game or two, when a couple of sportswriters began talking to Chabot in Hebrew.

From time to time, the *Hockey News* and other publications have referred to Chabot as a "Hall-of-Famer," but that's merely an assumption, not a fact. Chabot deserves Hall-of-Fame recognition, but he hasn't received it yet.

In 1994, Barry Parker, the man who married Chabot's granddaughter, wrote to the Hockey Hall of Fame in Toronto from Kelowna, British Columbia. He pleaded for posthumous recognition of Chabot and listed some of the great goaltender's accomplishments.

1. His career goals-against average (2.04) is fourth best in league history and is lower than any other goaltender's not inducted into the Hall.
2. His career shutouts total is eighth best in league history and is higher than any other goaltender's not inducted into the Hall.
3. His career shutout percentage is third highest in league history and is higher than any other goaltender's not inducted into the Hall.

4. Each winner of the Vezina Trophy prior to 1935 has been inducted into the Hall of Fame. Lorne Chabot won the Vezina Trophy in 1935 with a 1.83 goals-against average. A further fourteen subsequent winners of the Vezina Trophy have been inducted into the Hall.

Mr. Parker's plea on behalf of his wife's grandfather is supported by Royd Beamish, former sports editor of the Port Arthur *News-Chronicle*. In his submission to the Hockey Hall of Fame, Beamish writes: "Lorne Chabot toiled in the NHL vineyards in those early days when rewards were small and fame a fleeting thing. He was not only one of the world's finest goaltenders, but he was a great sportsman as well. I believe he deserves the recognition that has so long been withheld from him and is a fit and proper candidate for the Hockey Hall of Fame."

Amen.

Was Cook the Greatest Right Winger?

WHEN Bill Cook died in Kingston, Ontario, in the summer of 1986, he was hailed as the greatest right winger ever to play for the New York Rangers. He played alongside brother Bun and Frank Boucher — from the very first game — on a line that performed brilliantly for many seasons.

Cook was a well-traveled 30 — "a seasoned pro," the writers called him — when he joined the Rangers for their inaugural season in 1926. He'd been through the First World War, enlisting at age 17, and had survived battles at Ypres, Vimy Ridge, the Somme, and Flanders. He had seen postwar service in North

Russia, having been recruited to help put down Bolshevism, which was struggling to get a foothold after the revolution. Cook wore a .45 on his hip and carried a long Russian rifle. He scouted enemy lines on snowshoes and wore a white sheet over his body as camouflage. Many were killed, and Cook was described by a fellow soldier as "one of the bravest men I have ever seen." He was still fighting in Russia six months after the Armistice ended the war. If they'd been smart, the Russians would have kept him around as a hockey expert. If they had, perhaps the game would have flourished in Russia long before it did.

After the war, he took advantage of a Canadian government program for land grants in Saskatchewan. He took a half section adjoining his brother Bun's property.

Bill and his younger brother starred for Saskatoon in the Western Hockey League, and when the Rangers began recruiting players for an NHL expansion team, Bill Cook was happy to turn in his bib overalls for a Ranger uniform. He was the first player signed.

With Bun in tow, he arrived in New York and immediately became a team leader, creating many more "firsts" while wearing Ranger livery. He became the club's first captain. In the Rangers' first game, Cook scored the first goal — and first winning goal — in Rangers' history. It came on a pass from Bun, who earned his nickname after a Manhattan reporter wrote that he was "quick as a bunny."

Bill Cook, on the strength of 33 goals and 4 assists for 37 points during his first season, became the first Ranger to win the Art Ross Trophy as the NHL scoring champ. He captured the award again in 1932–33 and helped lead the Rangers to their second Stanley Cup.

When he retired at age 39, Cook had accumulated 228 goals and was the Ranger leader in goals for six of his 11 seasons. It's amazing that someone from his era still ranks number seven among all-time Ranger goal scorers. For comparison's sake, the record shows that Cook scored his 228 goals in 475 games, whereas Walt Tkaczuk, a modern-era star who compiled 227 career goals, played in 945 games.

Frank Boucher, who spent 31 years in New York as a player,

coach, and manager of the Rangers, once said, "Bill was the finest all-round player in Ranger history. And he's my choice as the best right winger hockey ever knew — despite the fact that others disagree and give their votes to Rocket Richard or Gordie Howe. I say Cook topped them both."

After his playing days, Cook made two triumphant returns to Madison Square Garden. In 1968, he helped close out the old Garden and usher in the new. "They brought me back because I scored the first goal in the old Madison Square Garden," he told reporters. "Then they gave me a puck and sent me out on the ice to put one in the net to christen the new Garden. Now that was quite an honor."

In January 1986, he was back again to receive the fourth annual Ranger Alumni Association Award. Once more, Cook was involved in another "first." It marked the first time that the award was voted upon by the over 400 members of the Ranger Alumni Association. Cook, almost 90 then, was the overwhelming choice. He received a standing ovation when he stepped out on the ice and received a framed replica of his old Ranger blue jersey from Ranger captain Barry Beck and an original oil painting of himself in action.

Hall-of-Famer Joe Primeau, as a member of the famed Toronto "Kid Line" of Primeau, Conacher, and Jackson, battled the Rangers' trio of the Cooks and Boucher on many occasions. Primeau held Cook in the highest regard. "Oh, he was a terrific hockey player," he said. "Nobody fooled around with Bill because he was tough — real tough. As for grading the right wingers in hockey in my day, I was always partial to my linemate Charlie Conacher. But Bill was the best we ever played against."

Taffy Was the First

I'T'S always fun to be first at anything, and Clarence "Taffy" Abel is remembered as the first U.S.-born and -trained player to perform in the NHL. Born in 1900, Taffy didn't play in his first organized hockey game until he was 18. But he proved to be a natural on skates and starred as an amateur while living in his hometown of Sault Ste. Marie, Michigan. By the time he was 23, he was a member of the U.S. Olympic hockey team and was chosen to take the Olympic oath and carry the Stars and Stripes in the opening ceremonies at Chamonix, France. His strong play on the open-air rink, with boards a foot high, helped the U.S. to four straight victories over European teams en route to the championship game against Canada. Despite an American loss to the Toronto Granites, Taffy's brilliance at the Olympics, especially against the Canadians, many of whom went on to play in the NHL, convinced him that he possessed the skills to become a first-rate defenseman in the professional ranks.

He was an original Ranger and teamed up with Ching Johnston (each weighed about 225 pounds) to provide New York with a rock solid defense. However, Abel showed little interest in signing the first pro contract he'd ever seen. When first approached by Ranger manager Conn Smythe, Abel hemmed and hawed. Smythe would later state: "Johnston was a tough bargainer but Abel was even tougher. I went to Minneapolis where they both were playing in the old semipro league there. I negotiated with Abel on a train that was about to pull away from the station. He kept holding back and suddenly the train gave a lurch. I jumped up and locked the door of my stateroom and stood in front of it. I said, 'Taffy, the money's good, you'll love New York, and if you don't sign this contract at once, you'll be stuck with me for the next 250 miles, which is the next stop.' He said, 'Okay, Mr. Smythe, hand me the pen.' He scrawled something on the bottom line, threw on his coat, said he'd see me at training camp, and leaped from the moving train. It's a wonder he didn't break a leg."

The Old Man Takes Over

N O book on the Rangers would be complete without the tale of Lester Patrick's famous stint in goal — in the Stanley Cup playoffs.

It happened on April 7, 1928, in the second game of the Stanley Cup finals between the Rangers and the Montreal Maroons. The Rangers were forced to play all of the games in Montreal because the circus had taken over the Garden.

Early in the second period, Montreal's Nels Stewart rifled a shot that struck Ranger goalie Lorne Chabot over the eye. He fell to the ice unconscious. Chabot was carried off on a stretcher, and, since teams didn't carry backup goalies, Lester Patrick, New York's 44-year-old manager, was forced to find a substitute. But where? He asked Montreal manager Eddie Gerrard if he could use Ottawa Senator goalie Alex Connell, who happened to be at the game.

"Are you crazy," Gerrard replied. "That guy's too good."

"How about Hugh McCormick?" McCormick was also at the game. He'd just completed an outstanding season for a London, Ontario, team.

"Nah. I don't want you using him, either."

Referee Mike Rodden gave Patrick 10 minutes to find someone to fill the Ranger net. Two of his players — Frank Boucher and Bill Cook, said, "Lester, looks like you're going to have to do it yourself."

Lester said, "I'm no goalie. Never have been. But I'll take Chabot's place if you guys promise to back-check like hell and clear all the rebounds."

The Rangers promised. They watched while their silver-haired manager laid out Chabot's soggy gear: the bulky pads, the belly protector, the skates that were too big. "Throw a couple of extra pairs of socks on, Lester," they advised him, "and don't forget your jock."

Out he waddled. The crowd at the Forum laughed, and then cheered. They sensed it took a lot of courage for the old man to step into a dangerous situation. They also sensed that this would be the turning point in the series. The Maroons had won the opener. If Lester faltered, New York's Cup chances were out the window.

But Lester didn't falter. He stopped 15 shots rated as "dangerous." He held the Maroons at bay on three occasions when his team played a man short. The second period ended scoreless.

The Rangers got a break 30 seconds into the third period when Bill Cook fired a long shot and Clint Benedict fanned on it.

Then Nels Stewart, one of the league's top scorers, knifed through the Ranger defense and drilled a shot to the corner. Somehow Patrick stopped it. Stewart tried again and was thwarted by Patrick's stick. The third time he raced in, he faked a shot and Patrick went down. Stewart calmly tucked the puck in behind him to tie the score.

Overtime!

The Maroons came crashing through. They were determined to take a stranglehold on the series, but the old man in the nets was taking their best shots, showing them up.

At the seven-minute mark, Ching Johnston grabbed a loose puck, saw clear ice ahead of him, and took off. He raced in on Benedict, threw a quick pass to Boucher. Red light! Game over!

Lester Patrick was mobbed by his players. Bill Cook noticed the sweat pouring down his face and complimented him on his "acrobatic performance." But when Cook and others, perhaps in jest, suggested he stage an encore in game three, he said, "No way, boys. It was all I could do to survive tonight."

Patrick's gallant stand was the turning point of the series. Goaltender Joe Miller was recruited to play in the games that remained. Miller, who would fashion a dismal 24-90 record in four NHL seasons, turned out to be a spectacular replacement.

He allowed only three goals in the remaining three games and was a huge factor in New York's initial Cup victory.

The story of Miller's relief work in his first and only playoffs is a great one. But Miller's name is seldom mentioned whenever the finals of '28 are discussed. All the kudos are reserved for Lester Patrick and his fabulous feat that turned the tide.

A Cup for the Rangers in '33

THE 1932–33 season in the NHL was an unusual one. It was the season John S. Hammond resigned as president of the New York Rangers and was replaced by William F. Carey. Thousands in New York were unemployed and almost broke. As a result, the price of tickets to games at the Garden was reduced by one-third. Balcony seats went for 40 cents, while rinkside ducats cost two dollars. The bargain prices attracted a crowd of over 15,000 for a game between the Rangers and the Americans. Attendance plummeted elsewhere around the league. Only 2,000 fans turned out in Detroit for a Red Wings' game against the Americans, and 4,000 paid in Chicago one night with Toronto, the defending Stanley Cup champions, providing the opposition.

At the end of the 48-game schedule, Bill Cook of the Rangers led all goal scorers with 28. He added 22 assists for 50 points, good enough to win the individual scoring title by six points over Harvey Jackson of Toronto.

The Rangers replaced tiny goaltender John Ross Roach (five foot five, 130 pounds) with Scottish-born Andy Aikenhead. Roach had skidded downhill after a spectacular performance in the 1929 playoffs, when he won his first three playoff starts for New York — all by shutouts. After a third-place finish in the

American Division in 1932–33, the Rangers sparkled in the play-offs, defeating Canadiens in two games, 8–5 in goals, Detroit in two games, 6–3 in goals, and Toronto in the best-of-five final, three games to one. Aikenhead emerged as the top playoff goalie with two shutouts and a 1.63 average, while four Rangers topped the playoff scoring parade — Cecil Dillon (eight goals in eight games), Murray Murdoch, Bill Cook, and Art Somers.

The Rangers had the advantage of being fresh and eager for their final series versus Toronto. The Leafs had eliminated Boston in a game that began on April 3 and ended on April 4. Little Ken Doraty, an obscure winger, scored five minutes into the sixth overtime period, at 2:30 in the morning, to win the game for Toronto 1–0. The weary Leafs left immediately for New York to play the well-rested Rangers. Ranger fans cheered lustily when their favorites captured the opener 5–1, but the booing rattled the roof when it was announced that the circus was moving into the Garden and the remaining games would be played back in Toronto. Lester Patrick tried to reassure Ranger supporters, stating, "Don't worry. We'll win this series in three straight games. We'll come back from Toronto with the Cup."

He was almost right. New York captured game two by a 3–1 score. Earl Seibert, the newcomer, rushed his way through the entire Toronto club to score an unassisted goal in the third period.

Doraty, the pesky little wingman, came up with another big effort in game three, scoring twice. The Leafs avoided elimination with a 3–2 victory.

Game four was scoreless through three periods and required sudden-death overtime. Suddenly Levinsky and Thoms, two Leaf stars, found themselves sharing space in the penalty box. Bill Cook grabbed a pass from Butch Keeling, lifted the puck over former Ranger goalie Lorne Chabot in the Toronto net, and scored the Cup-winning goal.

Ranger rearguard Ivan (Ching) Johnston, when asked to recall the triumph, remembers how furious the Leafs were at the finish. "Oh, Lord, they were sore," he chuckled. "Sore at those game officials. You see, there was a new rule, a really silly rule, in the books that season. A player couldn't raise his hands above his head or in front of his face to protect himself from a flying puck or stick. Instinctively, I did that early in the overtime and I was given a two-minute minor. While I sat in the penalty box, one of the Leafs did something similar and he was waved off. I guess the referee was attempting to even things up, even though the Leafs already had one man in the box. That's when Cook and Keeling took over. A few seconds later, Bill Cook snapped up Butch Keeling's pass and whipped the puck into the net past Chabot. We were ecstatic but those Leafs were boiling mad. No wonder the officials scurried off the ice the moment the winning goal was scored."

Don't Wake the Coach

WHEN the Rangers traveled by Pullman during the first three decades of their existence, the long train rides led to a spirit of togetherness that is not often matched by their modern-day counterparts. One such ride terminated in Ottawa one night. As the train pulled into Union Station, manager Lester Patrick spoke to his players. "Gentlemen, after we play the game tonight, we will return to this Pullman for the return trip to New York. We'll depart at 3:30 a.m. when hopefully you'll all be asleep in your bunks. The railway folks have notified me that the water supply may be frozen by nightfall because of the frigid temperatures outside. So please relieve yourselves before you return to the station, otherwise you'll have to pee in a bucket that will be provided."

After the game, which the Rangers won easily, the players found their way across the Ottawa River to Hull, Quebec. The bar they wound up in apparently had a closing hour that coincided with the crack of dawn. Sometime after 2:00 a.m., the players suddenly recalled Lester's words about the 3:30 a.m. departure.

Somewhat inebriated, and having shattered their normal curfew, they hustled back to their Pullman. "Whatever you do, don't wake Lester," they cautioned each other as they tiptoed through the car to their berths.

"I've got to take a leak," muttered big Butch Keeling. "And I don't know where the bloody pail is that Lester talked about."

"Be quiet," his mates admonished him. "Hold it until morning."

Came the dawn and the train was rattling along the tracks, headed for New York. Frank Boucher arose and entered the dining car where he joined Lester Patrick at a table.

"Mr. Boucher," said Lester. "The most amazing thing happened during the night. Are you aware that Butch Keeling walks in his sleep?"

"No, I'm not aware of that," replied Boucher. "Oh, it's fact," said Lester. "I learned about it during the wee small hours. The door to my compartment flew open and Mr. Keeling tiptoed in. I heard him whisper, 'Shhh. Don't wake Lester.' Then he proceeded to take a leak on the floor right next to me. The poor man must have been sleepwalking, don't you think? Otherwise he would have used the pail the railway kindly provided. Then Mr. Keeling left my compartment, after admonishing me again, 'Don't wake Lester.'"

Boucher kept a straight face. What would his manager say next?

At that point, Lester broke into peals of laughter. Tears sprang from his eyes as he said, "Frank, it was a hoot." He held up two fingers. "Butch missed me by that much. If he wasn't sleepwalking, do you suppose he was trying in some unspoken manner to communicate his feelings towards me as his coach?"

That did it. Boucher erupted in mirth and their combined howls of laughter filled the dining car.

Hall Doors Closed to Kerr

THE question is often asked but never answered: why isn't David Alexander Kerr in the Hockey Hall of Fame? Ranger fans say he — like Lorne Chabot — has been overlooked for far too long.

Oldtimers will tell you that Davey, a cocky little guy with the eyes of a hawk and the hands of a magician, was one of the best, if not *the* best goalie in the NHL from 1934 to 1941.

Kerr, a Toronto native who played on a Montreal Allan Cup–winning team from Montreal in 1929, moved to the Montreal Maroons of the NHL for the 1930–31 season, but didn't become a full-time netminder with the Maroons until the 1933–34 season. He was outstanding in a two-game playoff series against the Rangers that season, allowing just one goal.

When Lester Patrick's club tumbled into the league cellar early the following season, Patrick purchased Kerr from the Maroons for $10,000. There was an immediate improvement, and Kerr was a Ranger hero for the next seven years.

He was never more brilliant than during the 1937 playoffs when New York advanced to the Cup finals against Detroit. The Rangers eliminated Toronto two games to none in the opening round. Kerr had a shutout in the opening game and allowed just one goal in the second match. In the follow-up series against the Maroons, Kerr was sensational in the first game, registering a 1–0 shutout. He finished with a 4–0 shutout in game two, eliminating the punchless Maroons.

In the finals, Kerr's Rangers rolled to a 5–1 victory in the opening game. Kerr was slightly off form in game two, a 4–1 loss, but he bounced back with a 1–0 shutout in game three, and suffered a heartbreaking loss in game four (1–0). In the deciding fifth game, rookie Detroit goaltender Earl Robertson matched Kerr's brilliance and the Red Wings skated off with a 3–0 victory and the Stanley Cup.

Kerr could only shake his head in disbelief. He'd registered four shutouts in nine playoff games and a 1.11 goals-against average — and had nothing to show for it.

His finest season was 1939–40 when he was the only NHL goaltender to allow an average of less than two goals per game (1.60). As a result, he won the Vezina Trophy and was named to the first All-Star team.

In the opening round of the playoffs against the defending champion Boston Bruins, Kerr rang up three shutouts in the six-game series, won by New York, four games to two. The Rangers followed up with a four-games-to-two triumph over the Toronto Maple Leafs, and Davey Kerr finally had his name on the Stanley Cup.

His final career stats were impressive — 51 shutouts and a 2.17 goals-against average in 426 games.

Rangers in Hockey Doubleheader

IN the fall of 1937, the New York Rangers and the New York Americans journeyed to Saskatoon, Saskatchewan, for a pre-season game. It would be the first match involving two NHL clubs to be played in the new arena in that hockey hotbed. Tickets for the event were gobbled up within minutes of going on sale and thousands of fans in line were left empty-handed. The promoters huddled with the managers of the two hockey clubs and decided that two games would meet the demand — and fatten their pocketbooks — so two separate games were played — on the same day! The referee for both matches was young Clarence Campbell, who would go on to become a Rhodes scholar in England, a war-crimes prosecutor in Germany, and eventually, president of the NHL.

The Patricks — What a Family!

I
T'S true that no family has delivered as many players to the NHL as the Sutter clan of Viking, Alberta. To have six Sutters (out of seven) make it to the top level of the game is a story that Ripley would have loved.

But there's a second family that has contributed as much or more manpower and talent to the game as the lads from Viking. Add up the number of Patricks who've excelled on the ice and in the game's front offices and one can readily understand why the Patrick fraternity is called "Hockey's Royal Family."

Patriarch Lester Patrick was born in Drummondville, Quebec, in 1883, 10 years before the Stanley Cup (purchased in England for 50 bucks) arrived in Canada to be put up for competition. By the time Lester was 20, he was regarded as one of the game's greatest stars and its first rushing defenseman. His brother Frank, two years younger, was almost as good.

In 1909, Lester and his brother Frank joined the Renfrew Creamery Kings and were paid "astronomical" salaries — $3,000 for Lester and $2,000 for Frank. When Renfrew failed to win the Stanley Cup and the team was about to fold, the Patrick brothers moved west. In 1911, they supervised the construction of the first artificial ice arenas in Canada in Vancouver and Victoria. They had both played on artificial ice during exhibition games booked at the St. Nicholas rink in New York. In 1912, they introduced their own professional league — the Pacific Coast Hockey Association — and Frank began raiding eastern clubs for players.

In 1926, unable to compete financially with pro hockey in the East, the Patricks orchestrated a remarkable deal with the newly expanded NHL, selling their entire stable of Western Hockey League players to NHL clubs. Lester was invited to take over the new franchise in New York and delivered a Stanley Cup to grateful Ranger fans in the team's second season. By the time he won two more, he had become a Ranger legend.

Frank Patrick was a shrewd executive and innovator. He and his brother Lester conceived several changes to the game (including blue lines) that appealed to the fans. Another Patrick innovation was the numbering of players. A third was the introduction of playoff games. Then came penalty shots, the awarding of points for assists, and complete line changes. Frank later served as coach of the Boston Bruins and business manager of the Montreal Canadiens. His son Joe played hockey at Harvard and with the Boston Olympics.

Lester's husky sons, Lynn and Murray (Muzz) Patrick, played for the Rangers in the late '30s and starred on the Ranger club that captured the Stanley Cup in 1940. After their playing days, both went on to coach and manage in the NHL. Lynn coached the Rangers from December 1948 through the 1949–50 season. Muzz coached them briefly in the mid-fifties and managed the club from 1955 to 1964.

Lynn went on to coach the Boston Bruins for five seasons, then moved to the front office. With the initial NHL expansion, he became the first general manager of the St. Louis Blues in 1966, coached the team briefly on three occasions, and retired as senior vice-president in 1977.

Dick Patrick (Murray's son), after a career in college hockey, has served as president of the Washington Capitals for several seasons. Lynn's sons Craig and Glenn both enjoyed NHL careers (Craig for eight seasons, Glenn for three). Craig later served as assistant general manager and assistant coach of the 1980 gold-medal-winning U.S. Olympic team before joining the New York Rangers as director of operations later that year. On June 14, 1981, he became the youngest general manager in Ranger history. Now 51, he is the executive vice-president and general manager of the Pittsburgh Penguins. Craig earned wide respect after guiding the Penguins to back-to-back Stanley Cups ('91 and '92) and four Division titles.

Surely the tradition of Patricks in hockey will continue. Let's hope youthful members of this "Royal Family" will pursue careers that will take them across the ice and into the boardrooms of NHL teams. One thing is almost certain: the fathers and grandfathers who've preceded them have set standards that may be impossibly high for a modern-day Patrick to surpass.

Winning in Wartime

WHEN the Second World War was declared in September 1939, the NHL was only a few days away from opening its 48-game schedule and there were indications that brilliant careers would soon be interrupted by the booming guns in Europe.

Seven teams competed for league honors in the 1939–40 season, with the Boston Bruins showing the most clout, finishing atop the standings with 67 points, three more than the second-place Rangers. The Bruins' Kraut Line of Milt Schmidt, Bobby Bauer, and Woody Dumart made history by copping the first three positions in the individual scoring race. The Rangers' Bryan Hextall led all players in goals scored with 24.

It was the season Lester Patrick stepped down as coach of the Rangers, replaced by Frank Boucher. Boucher was delighted with the play of his Colville-Shibicky-Colville line and equally impressed with the performance of the Hextall-Watson-Patrick combination. By mid-January, the Rangers had lost only three games and had gone a record 19 games without a defeat. After dropping a 2–1 decision to Chicago, they ran off another five wins before losing again. One loss in 25 games was simply incredible. Dave Kerr, a Ranger goalie since 1934, was largely responsible for the streak. He had the agility of a gymnast and a tongue that never stopped. He'd shout instructions at his teammates, exhorting them to make the proper plays. Kerr fashioned a 1.60 goals-against average to go with his eight shutouts — both league highs. He won his only Vezina Trophy that season.

The Rangers and the Bruins played a pair of games late in the season. One ended in a scoreless tie, the other was a 2–1 victory for Boston. For the third straight season, the Bruins compiled the best record in the NHL.

The playoff system was quirky and generous in those days and included every team but one — the last-place Montreal Canadiens. The Rangers faced the defending champion Bruins in the first round of the playoffs, which may have made sense in that era but would be incomprehensible today. Dave Kerr, with a shutout, was the opening-game hero at Madison Square Garden. The Rangers dropped a 4–0 goose egg on the visitors.

The Bruins roared back with two straight victories, 4–2 and 4–3. Then it was Kerr's turn to shine again. Before the largest crowd of the season in New York, 16,504, he registered his second shutout in a 1–0 victory. Two nights later he did it again, winning 1–0 and picking up his third shutout of the series. New Yorkers had never seen such shot blocking. The Rangers ousted the Bruins from the Stanley Cup hunt with a 4–1 triumph in game five. The victory earned them a bye into the finals.

Toronto survived by eliminating Chicago and Detroit, only to face off against the Rangers for the Cup, with the first two games slated for New York on April 2 and 3.

In the opener, Ranger defenseman Alf Pike scored the winner in overtime and Bryan Hextall was the star of game two, won by New York 6–2. Hextall, held scoreless for seven games, suddenly exploded for three goals and was virtually unstoppable. His performance was still being cheered, postgame, even as the boards were being removed to make way for the incoming circus.

Back in Toronto, the Leafs rebounded with a 2–1 victory. Hank Goldup beat Kerr with seven minutes to play for the winning goal.

In game four, the Rangers missed Alex Shibicky, out with a sprained ankle, and were shut out by Turk Broda and the Leafs 3–0. Shibicky was back for game five but his tender ankle gave out and he was unable to finish the match. Murray Patrick won the game for New York (2–1) in the second overtime period with a shot that eluded Broda's grasp.

Facing elimination, the desperate Leafs jumped into a 2–0 lead in game six. In the third period, the Rangers rallied. Neil

Colville and Alf Pike scored goals to tie the score and Bryan Hextall potted the winner in 2:07 of overtime, after taking a pass from Phil Watson.

Manager Lester Patrick proudly posed for a photographer alongside his sons Murray and Lynn. For the first time, the Stanley Cup would display the names of four members of one family — Lester and Frank Patrick, and Lester's sons Murray and Lynn. Over half a century later, in 1991, another Patrick name would be added to the famous trophy after Lynn's son Craig managed the Pittsburgh Penguins to a Cup triumph over Chicago.

After winning the Cup in 1940, the Rangers celebrated back at their hotel — the Royal York. They drank some beer from Lord Stanley's big basin and smoked cigars. The following day about half the team boarded a train for New York, others headed off to western Canada. New Yorkers were pleased with the triumph but there was no big celebration. Nobody considered holding a victory parade or presenting championship rings. The players were given gold watches worth about $30.

The rings would come 50 years later. In 1990, Ranger general manager Neil Smith decided the seven surviving members of the 1940 championship squad had waited long enough. He presented each of them with an expensive Stanley Cup ring to mark the anniversary of a memorable moment in Ranger team history.

To show his appreciation, Clint Smith dug out his old Ranger jersey — number 10 — and presented it to Neil Smith. "Maybe it'll bring you luck," the oldtimer said. The Ranger manager had the jersey framed and placed on a wall in his office. Within four seasons and after a 54-year drought, his team had captured the Stanley Cup.

Ranger Streak Ends on a Sour Note

FRANK Boucher was a huge success in his first season as coach of the Rangers (1939–40). His team lost a mere 11 games out of 48 and his goaltender, Dave Kerr, was phenomenal, allowing only 77 goals for a 1.6 goals-against average. Kerr won the Vezina by 21 goals over Boston's ace netminder, Frank Brimsek.

That was the season the Rangers embarked on an undefeated streak that stretched to 10, then 15, then 19 games. The 19th game in the Ranger streak was played in Toronto on January 13 — a 4–1 New York victory. The following night at the Chicago Stadium, after a long train ride from Canada, Kerr and his mates suited up to play the Black Hawks, a team that was getting splendid goaltending from rookie Paul Goodman, who played in 31 of his 52 career games that season.

Prior to the game, Boucher took Davey Kerr aside and gave him explicit instructions. "If the Rangers happen to be trailing by a goal late in the game," he said, "watch for my signal. I may pull you from the net even though the play is in progress. Got it?"

"Got it, coach," Kerr replied.

Up until that time, a goalie had never been pulled from the net for another attacker unless there was a faceoff. But there was no rule stating he couldn't be pulled while play was in progress and Boucher was determined to try it. The move might surprise and confuse the Hawks and lead to the tying goal.

Sure enough, the Rangers fell behind Chicago by 2–1. They outshot and outskated the Hawks but they couldn't put the puck past Goodman.

With less than two minutes to play, and with the puck in the Chicago zone, Boucher signaled Kerr and the goalie made a beeline for the bench. Ott Heller replaced him on the ice and hustled after the puck.

While this was happening, Lester Patrick, the Ranger manager, was standing between the players' benches. He didn't notice, nor did he anticipate that Kerr might leave his net. But he did see Heller, the extra player, leap into the action.

"Too many men!" he shouted at Boucher. "Frank, you've got too many men on the ice."

Paul Thompson, the Chicago coach, heard Lester's warning cry and began to shout at the referee. "Too many men on the ice!" he screamed over and over.

The referee took a quick count and blew his whistle. "Penalty to New York," he announced.

Boucher threw his hands in the air in frustration. Then he pointed at the empty net. "I pulled my goalie, you dummies," he muttered, shaking his head in anguish.

The referee waved off the penalty, Lester Patrick came over to apologize to Boucher for ruining a unique bit of strategy, and Paul Thompson sighed with relief, for the Ranger pressure in the Chicago zone had been intense.

The Hawks held on to win the game by a 2–1 score and the longest undefeated streak in Ranger history was over.

Hockey is always a game of what-ifs. What if the Rangers had tied the score in the final seconds that night in Chicago and kept their streak alive with a victory or a tie? They went on to win five more games before suffering another loss. Their undefeated streak would have ended after 25 games, not 19.

First on TV

H ERE'S one for trivia fans. Name the year when television first covered a hockey game, and which two teams were involved? Take a guess. Was it 1960, 1950, or 1940?

You'll find the answer in this account of a game played

between the Montreal Canadiens and the New York Rangers. The game was played at Madison Square Garden on February 15, 1940. That night, fans who couldn't attend the game were able to watch it at home, thanks to a miraculous new invention called television. Only a few hundred people witnessed the debut of NHL hockey on an experimental TV station set up by NBC because there were only about 300 TV sets scattered throughout the city. Their screens were a minuscule seven inches wide.

At Madison Square Garden, a single cameraman followed the play, and the announcer who called the game was Skip Waltz, although he often used the name Bill Allen.

Ranger fans remember the 1939–40 season, not for television, but for their team's marvellous accomplishments on ice. It was one of New York's finest seasons. The Rangers played a record 19 games without defeat. In the opening playoff round, they downed Boston, first-place finishers, in six games to earn a bye into the finals. New York then ousted Toronto in the final round, four games to two, and captured the Stanley Cup on April 13 at Maple Leaf Gardens.

It was years before NHL officials welcomed TV cameras to hockey games. When the CBC began televising games from Montreal and Toronto during the 1952–53 season, NHL president Clarence Campbell called television "the greatest menace in the entertainment world."

The Rangers figured prominently in U.S. network television's second foray into hockey in the 1950s. New York hosted the first CBS telecast on January 5, 1957, and defeated Chicago 4–1. The Rangers were involved in four of the nine games telecast by CBS that season and won three of them. The following year, CBS produced an *NHL Game of the Week* with Bud Palmer and Fred Cusick in the broadcast booth. In 1960 (with Palmer at the Olympics), your author joined play-by-play man Cusick as color commentator. Prior to each intermission, the color commentator would leave his perch in the broadcast booth, hustle down a back stairwell to rinkside, throw on a pair of skates and interview players on the ice. These segments often included demonstrations of hockey's fundamentals by the stars of that era.

Lester's Son Lynn
Not Made for Hockey

LYNN Patrick, born and brought up in Victoria, British Columbia, where the weather is so mild that entire winters pass without a single day for outdoor skating, didn't have a chance in hockey. He'd never be much of a player and never be a pro.

That's what his father thought. That's what his father told him.

Lester Patrick, manager of the New York Rangers, knew his son Lynn had visions of being a big star. But he told him to be realistic. He'd had so little practise time — a few hours now and then on the ice of the indoor rink in Victoria — which burned down in 1929, leaving Lynn heartbroken — that he'd never be good enough for professional hockey.

So Lynn turned to other sports. He became a track star and an all-star rugby player. In basketball, he paced the Victoria Blue Ribbons to the Canadian championship. He moved to Montreal to play professional football and became a pass-catching wizard for the Winged Wheelers. In 1934, he joined the Winnipeg Blue Bombers and broke a record by catching a 68-yard touchdown pass — the longest pass completion in Canadian football history.

That fall, he begged his famous father for a hockey tryout even though he'd been off skates from age 17 to 22 and had played only one season of hockey with the Montreal Royals. Lester continued to tell him he didn't have a chance, but agreed to take him to camp.

That's where two Ranger stars, Bill Cook and Frank Boucher, gave him a timely boost. They disagreed with the father's assessment of the son. They could see young Patrick's potential and told their boss he'd be wise to sign the young man for the Rangers.

Lester reluctantly signed Lynn to a contract. But he had second thoughts about the wisdom of his decision when Lynn first donned a Ranger uniform for the 1934–35 NHL season.

"He was pretty terrible," Lester would write in his memoirs. "I can hear it now, as it rolled down from the top balcony of Madison Square Garden — that insistent demand, chanted over and over. 'Take him out! Take him out!' That cry stabbed me — hard.

"I knew Lynn was no star, believe me. But I had made up my mind I was going to see the redheaded kid through. And before long, within a couple of seasons, I began to profit handsomely because of the brilliant play of my son. He shot many vital goals in the amazing march of a team that was a 50:1 shot to get into the Stanley Cup finals in 1937 after finishing last the year before."

Lynn was a member of the 1940 Rangers when they won the Stanley Cup. It is a matter of record that he was the leading goalscorer in the NHL in 1941–42. The next season was his best. He finished with 22 goals and 61 points. In '42, he was selected at left wing on the All-Star team.

Lester Patrick has enjoyed many triumphs in professional hockey. "High on my list of thrills," he once said, "was witnessing Lynn's determination to succeed. Nothing has given me the flush of satisfaction that came with the realization that my bungling but persistent redheaded son had made the grade to hockey stardom."

Why the Rangers Hit the Skids

"THAT was a great little team we had in 1940," former Ranger Art Coulter once said. "We could have beaten anybody. We should have won three Stanley Cups."

Why then did the team with so much promise sink to the league basement within two years and remain there for the next four seasons?

Many reasons for the Rangers' demise during the forties have been advanced. Lester Patrick was accused of selling off top prospects on the Ranger farm team to other NHL clubs who'd lost players to the Canadian and American armed forces.

Every spring, the Rangers lost their home ice for playoff games because greedy moguls booked the circus into Madison Square Garden.

"We lost two Stanley Cups in Atlantic City," Art Coulter states. "When the circus took over our rink, Lester Patrick moved the team to Atlantic City where he worked our butts off. He figured we were fat and sassy, when we were down to skin and bone. We skated and skated when we should have been relaxing, saving our strength for the playoff games. We were worn out, exhausted."

The team was hard hit by the war. Muzz Patrick, Kilby MacDonald, Art Coulter, Alex Shibicky, and Neil and Mac Colville all joined the armed services. Other veterans quit after salary disputes with penurious Lester Patrick.

Finally, there was the story of a mysterious hex placed on the team by an angry competitor, Red Dutton. Dutton, then manager of the rival New York Americans, is said to have blamed Ranger management for forcing his team to disband in 1942. Dutton, it was alleged, vowed his personal curse would keep the Rangers from winning the Stanley Cup "as long as I'm alive." He died in 1987, so his hex was a strong one. Seven years after his death, the Rangers finally won their next Stanley Cup.

John Halligan, public relations director of the Rangers for 24 years, made an effort in 1985 to verify the story of the Dutton hex. He discussed the matter with Dutton at the NHL All-Star game in Calgary. "Dutton was a very alert guy and told me the story of the hex was a lot of newspaper talk," says Halligan. "That to me indicated there was no truth to the story. Then he winked at me and said, 'John, sometimes the newspapers get things right.'"

Buzinski Was a Beautiful Bust

THE Rangers have employed some of hockey's best goaltenders over the years — Dave Kerr, Terry Sawchuk, Eddie Giacomin, and Mike Richter. They've also been stuck with two of the all-time worst.

The record books show that Steve Buzinski, a little man who weighed only 140 pounds, served a nine-game stint with Frank Boucher's Rangers during the 1942–43 season (wartime hockey).

"I thought I'd seen some lousy goaltending during my career in hockey," Boucher once recalled, "but all of the sieves I'd seen were aces compared to Buzinski. One night in Detroit, the Red Wings plastered nine goals past him in the first two periods. In the third period, Buzinski rushed from his net, caught the puck in his glove, and tumbled in an awkward heap on the ice. Ott Heller went over to help him up and heard Buzinski say, 'Just like pickin' cherries, Ott.'"

Lynn Patrick topped Boucher's story with one of his own.

"We were playing Toronto one night and when the Leafs scored an easy goal, Buzinski swooned to the ice as he did on an average of once every period. He lay there, apparently unconscious, while blood trickled from a tiny cut on his cheek. We turned to the referee and argued that he'd been hit by a Leaf stick by a player in the crease and the goal shouldn't count. The Leafs argued that it was a puck that did the damage.

Suddenly Buzinski sat bolt upright. "It was a stick, dammit," he shouted, and fell back unconscious again.

"All the players on the ice stopped arguing and started laughing. We even went over to the benches to tell the rest of the guys what had happened. Buzinski gave us enough funny moments to make up for all the pain he caused us. Well, almost . . .

"How did he fare in those nine games he played for us? Well, he gave up about six goals a game (5.89 goals-against average), which must be one of the highest in history."

In 1984, Buzinski was interviewed about his NHL career and admitted he'd made the remark about "pickin' cherries."

"But I have no recollection of that other incident where I suddenly woke up and claimed it was a stick that hit me. But it sounds like something I would do [laughs]. In wartime hockey, you had to keep your sense of humor."

"Steve was a beautiful little guy," said Boucher. "He was earnest and sincere and we all liked him tremendously. There was just one little problem. He couldn't stop a puck worth a damn."

No wonder he became known as Steve Buzinski — the Puck Goes Inski.

"The next season we had a goaltender who was just as bad — Ken McCauley from Edmonton. He played in all 50 games, including a 15–0 shellacking we took from Detroit — and finished with a goals-against average of 6.20."

The NHL record book reveals that McCauley and the Rangers won a mere six games in 1943–44 and allowed 310 goals, the most goals scored against an NHL team in league history. The mark would last until 1970–71, when the California Golden Seals, in 78 games, gave up 320 goals.

McCauley got off to the poorest start of any NHL goaltender. Fifteen seconds into his first game, Gus Bodnar of the Toronto Maple Leafs raced in and scored on him. It was the fastest goal ever scored by a rookie and the fastest goal ever given up by a rookie netminder.

Gambling Ranger Gets Lifetime Suspension

ONLY one major gambling scandal has marred major league hockey, and it made headlines almost 50 years ago. Billy Taylor, then a Ranger, was suspended from hockey for life by league president Clarence Campbell for associating with a Detroit gambler named James Tamer. Tamer, a paroled bank robber, was arrested in 1948 for bookmaking. When interrogated, Tamer began to sing about his relations with a pair of center-ice men, 29-year-old Taylor and 22-year-old Don Gallinger, a Boston Bruin.

Tamer said he had received a call from "a Boston player" informing him the Bruins were in rough shape for their next game against the Chicago Black Hawks. Milt Schmidt, Boston's captain, was badly hurt and Jack Crawford, an ace defenseman, would be attending a funeral. The caller said Boston's chances of winning the game were poor.

Tamer then relayed this information to a New York Ranger (Taylor) who instructed him to bet $500 on Chicago to win. The bet was lost when Boston won the hockey game 4–2.

Clarence Campbell made a full investigation and on March 9, a few days after famed radio announcer Walter Winchell named Taylor and Gallinger as the players involved, announced the lifetime suspension of the Rangers' Taylor, who had been traded to New York from the Bruins a couple of weeks earlier.

On the same day, Gallinger, who challenged Campbell to prove his guilt, was suspended "until further notice" and subsequently expelled from the game permanently. The suspensions were not lifted until 1970 when both men were middle-aged.

Gallinger, who initially denied any role in the affair and was convicted on the flimsiest of evidence, years later would admit that he bet $1,500 against his Bruins to win the Chicago game —

at 2:1 odds. With the score tied 2–2, he skated through the Hawk defense in the third period and set up the winning goal, thus blowing three thousand bucks.

Taylor and Gallinger were less fortunate than big Babe Pratt who played defense for the Rangers from 1935–36 until he was traded to Toronto midway through the 1942–43 season. Pratt was also a known gambler on hockey games. Late in his life, Pratt told hockey reporter Dick Beddoes, "We could always get action down in New York. Sweeney Schriner of the Americans and Teeder Kennedy of the Leafs would come to my room and we'd phone around to our contacts and get our money down."

In 1946, Pratt was suspended by NHL president Frank Calder for wagering on NHL games. Unlike Campbell, his successor, a man who gained fame by prosecuting Nazi war criminals, Calder proved to be a lenient magistrate. His sentence was a slap on the wrist to Pratt — a mere 16 days. Pratt's candid confession and his promise "not to do it again" impressed the league moguls and he was back in uniform after missing nine games. In 1966, he and Kennedy (who was never investigated or charged) were inducted into the Hockey Hall of Fame.

Ironically, many of the team owners who supported Campbell's suspension of Taylor and Gallinger half a century ago were among the biggest gamblers on the continent. Big Jim Norris, owner of the Black Hawks, was a pal of many underworld figures including Frankie Carbo, who was known to fix a prize-fight or two. Norris, Conn Smythe, Frank Selke, and other top hockey men owned racing stables, and Smythe's arena was a haven for gamblers. As a young boy, enjoying my first game at Maple Leaf Gardens, I witnessed huge sums of money being exchanged after a game in an area known as "the bullpen."

Perhaps the crowning irony is that Clarence Campbell, the man who castigated Taylor and Gallinger for their transgressions and barred them from the game, was himself found guilty in 1980 of bribing a Liberal Senator with $95,000 in return for his influence in getting a lease extended for a business called Sky Shops at a Montreal airport. Campbell, then 74 and in failing health, was fortunate to avoid a lengthy prison term. He was sentenced to a day in jail and fined $25,000.

Gallinger would say, "Campbell sure got better treatment than the son of a bitch gave me."

The Killer Says It Never Happened

ALL of us growing up with hockey followed the brilliant career of Rocket Richard. And most of us chuckled over the story of his one-sided battle with Ranger strongman Bob "Killer" Dill at Madison Square Garden one night. The Rocket knocked Dill unconscious — not once, but twice.

The Rangers counted on Dill, a tough kid from Minnesota, to deal with the troublesome Canadiens' superstar. Dill was instructed to challenge the Rocket, which he did, but before Dill could throw one of his famous "killer" punches, he found himself stretched out on the ice — out cold. Minutes later, his wits back in motion, Dill staggered to the penalty box where he turned and cursed the Rocket, who was sitting a few feet away. In those days, there was no barrier separating the penalty box inhabitants, and some say the owners wanted it that way. Some of the best hockey fights took place in the box — not on the ice. The Rocket's first language may have been French but he was familiar with all of Dill's English slurs and he reacted swiftly. He leaped at Dill and caught him with another haymaker. Down went the Killer — out cold for the second time.

It's been said that Dill, his reputation shot, never recovered from the humiliation of the Richard fiasco. His two-season career with the Rangers consisted of 76 games, 15 goals, 30 points, and 135 penalty minutes. Today, if he's remembered at all, it's for the beating he suffered at the hands of Richard.

Late in his life Dill would say, "It's a hell of a thing to be remembered for, especially since the incident never took place! Sure, the Rocket and I had a little set-to in that game and he knocked me down and I was groggy. And yes, we got penalties. In the box, I called him a dirty so-and-so and he reached over and punched me over the eye. It bled a little, enough for three stitches as I recall. But that was it. There was no second knockout. Geez, the reporters built it up and books have been written with the story about how I got beaten up that night. You'd think I'd been knocked out for 15 minutes the way it was told."

One reporter told Dill in 1970 that he'd never be able to set the record straight because nobody would believe him. He suggested that Dill tell people who ask, "Yessiree, man, the Rocket caught me with a couple of dandy punches that night. I had him scared, though. He was scared he'd killed me."

Dill didn't take kindly to the suggestion, didn't think it was funny. He did offer a final thought on the incident. "I could never figure out why the Rocket didn't set the record straight," he said. "He scored all those goals, won all those Cups. Why would he want to take credit for a phony fight, a knockout that never happened?"

Patrick's Coaching Nightmare

OLDTIME Ranger fans shudder when hockey talk shifts to the season of 1943–44. Coach Frank Boucher used 32 players that season, 14 of them for less than a dozen games, in a desperate effort to find a winning combination. Boucher, at 42, even came out of retirement and played in 15 games, scoring four goals and adding ten assists. He hadn't played in five seasons and still outscored 19 other players on his squad.

The Rangers won only six games of the 50 played and finished so deep in the basement, they were 26 points behind fifth-place Chicago.

Their most disastrous performance came on the night of January 23, 1944, in Detroit. Several records established in that match with the Red Wings are still in the *NHL Record Book and Guide*, including a mark for most consecutive goals scored — 15.

"Don't blame my coaching for that one," Frank Boucher used to tell people. He'd laugh and say, "That game was Lester Patrick's nightmare."

"How come?" he was asked. "You were behind the Ranger bench that season."

"I was, but not that night. You see, I got word just before the game that my brother had died in Ottawa. I told Lester I wanted to go home and he said he'd be happy to fill in for me for the Detroit game. Lester always loved to coach and this would be his final fling at it. Well, Detroit filled the net that night and walloped us 15–0. They scored 15 times and we didn't come close. They scored eight of their goals in the third period and Ken McAuley, our poor goaltender, came off the ice looking like he'd been through a meatgrinder. The guy should have been given a medal.

"Lester never coached another game in the NHL. What a way to go out!"

Garden Memories

I found his letter in the files at the Hockey Hall of Fame in Toronto. The writer was a hockey fan from bygone days — a Ranger fan — retired now and living in Sonoma, California. Sunny Sonoma. He signed his letter A.D. Suehsdorf.

He wrote the Hall, entrusting to its care a donation — a page from a Madison Square Garden program from the 1928–29 season, bearing the autographs of 20 famous players of that era.

He went on to reminisce about those early days of the NHL — and I'm glad he did.

He wrote fondly of "his" Madison Square Garden, the second one, located between Forty-ninth and Fiftieth Streets and Eighth and Ninth Avenues. In 1928–29, he was just a lad seeking autographs at the games and his goal was to obtain the signatures of all 130 players in the NHL.

But he wound up with more than autographs. Some players, like Ranger star Bill Cook, gave him sticks they no longer needed. "Cook's was slightly curved," he recalls, "and about a five lie." A Chicago rookie, Harold "Mush" March, signed his autograph book in 1929 and five years later sent him a bonus — the jersey he was wearing when he scored the overtime goal that won the Stanley Cup for the Hawks in 1934.

"Collecting autographs was exhilarating and not at all difficult," he writes. Hockey had not yet attracted the following it enjoys today. At the Garden, crowds of six or seven thousand were usual. Tickets — take your choice — could be purchased right up until game time. Only one of the Garden's wheezing old special cops (who had a way with words) ever gave him trouble: "Hey, kid! Beat it! No monograms allowed!"

In their well-pressed suits, their fly-front top coats and snap-brim fedoras, players of that time looked like young businessmen, until you got close enough to see the healing cuts and memorial scars that mark the business of hockey. I found them a good-natured lot. A smile, a joshing remark, a pleasantry always went with the signature. Chuck Gardiner of the Hawks, probably the finest goalie of his time, liked to add "Blind Tom" or "The Human Sieve" after his name. In due course I had my 130.

I remember these men fondly. Lots of ice time for fewer players may have made our hockey a slower game as did the lack of a red line (not yet a dawning idea in Frank Boucher's head). But in those days without helmets and masks, I think we saw our players more clearly as people. There was perhaps more room for the idiosyncratic people. Goalies Dolly Dolson and Flat Walsh favored plebeian cloth caps, which made them look like New York City cabdrivers. Herb Drury wore a beret. Others opted for the blue baseball caps: Tiny Thompson, Alex Connell, Bill Brydge, Normie Himes (to cover his prematurely bald pate), and Aurel Joliat, for whom knocking his cap off was an invitation to fight.

The Rangers' Ching Johnston's bald dome, sans helmet, shone like a beacon above his demonic smile which grew broader and wickeder as the conflict grew more strenuous.

As chance would have it, I saw the Quakers in two December defeats — 3–0 to the Americans and 4–2 to the Rangers. These were the seventh and eleventh games of the 15 straight losses. The game against the Amerks is recalled as the first NHL appearance of a 20-year-old goalie named Wilf Cude. Joe Miller had started in the Quaker nets. "Red Light" they called him and, to be sure, he was frequently scored on. By mid-game, the Americans had racked up two goals, certainly not a lot, but suddenly time was called. Miller was summoned to the bench and dismissed for the night. Young Cude lumbered onto the ice to take his place. These days, with the wear and tear of long schedules and the unnerving frequency of high-scoring games, substituting goalies is no big thing. Back then, it was stunning. A sympathetic murmur arose from the 5,000 fans. Given the overall futility of the Quakers, it seemed monstrously unfair to single out "Red Light" for ignominy. The Americans scored a third and final goal against Cude, so it could be said he was twice as effective as Miller. Cude would go on to play over seven, presumably happier, years with the Canadiens.

That season the visitors' dressing room was at the West 50th Street corner of the Garden, where, in those pre-Zamboni days, the ice-scraping crew shoveled its slush between periods, and where the circus elephants made their entrances and exits. I made my way there to catch the Quakers as they left the ice, and while waiting, struck up a conversation with a portly gent who was also waiting, though not for autographs. The players appeared and I managed to get Hib Milks, the only really first-rate player the team owned. His fury at the outcome of the game survives on my program in the stabs he made with my balky pen.

Meanwhile, the other players had disappeared into the dressing room. Then the door opened. My portly gent, evidently a team official, beckoned me in. I wanted autographs? Go to it.

In the citadel of the defeated, the air was pungent, tobacco reek mixing with the heat and steam from the showers. Players were peeling off their sodden uniforms, some sore and silent, some cracking wise, some simply bushed. The angular Cude was still in his pads, enduring the culture shock of his first big-league game. I made my rounds. They all signed willingly.

Later on I found there were other programs for other signatures, and I found that a courteous letter to a "Mush" March or a Georges Mantha would be rewarded with the scribbles of every man on the club. In due time I had my 130.

I loved these evenings at the Garden. Joe Basile's handsomely accoutred band tootled popular tunes in a bright and breezy style from a splendid location at the Ninth Avenue end. The unsold seats they represented would give the present management fits.

The teams appeared, walking herky-jerky with support from their sticks on land, but gliding like angels on the ice. The house lights went down, the rink lights came up, and in that great white glare those boldly colored uniforms wheeled and whirled on their swift and urgent errands: Boston's brown and gold, Detroit's red and white, the diagonal lettering on Ranger blue, the maroon Maroons favored by English-speaking Montreal, the fabulous red of the other Montreal's Flying

Frenchmen, and most spectacular of all, the Americans' astonishing stars and stripes. For a weak-ankled boy from New Jersey, it was a pageant beyond compare.

As we departed, game over, and a new crop of autographs to be savored, Joe Basile always struck up bandleader Isham Jones's "I'll See You in My Dreams." How right he was.

2

THE FRANK BOUCHER ERA

From the Mounties
to the Majors

U NLIKE most kids who grew up in Canada — kids who dreamed of one day wearing a colorful jersey belonging to an NHL team — young Frankie Boucher pictured himself wearing a much different uniform — the flame-red tunic of the Royal Canadian Mounted Police.

One day in 1919, 17-year-old Boucher left his $10-a-week job as an Ottawa office boy, met his 19-year-old pal Bill Kerr, and trotted off to a nearby recruiting station to join the Mounties. In May of that year, they found themselves en route to Regina, Saskatchewan, for three months of training.

Boucher was posted to the Lethbridge area. His duties required him to seek out opium smokers in Chinese communities, to search for liquor stills in southern Alberta, and occasionally to track down train robbers.

When he was off duty, the young constable found time for hockey. His skills on ice far surpassed his talents on horseback. Away from the barracks, he became an outstanding player with Lethbridge in the Alberta Senior League. By 1921, he decided it was more fun, and more profitable, to chase hockey pucks than it was to chase bad guys with loaded guns. He turned in his red tunic — paying $50 to buy his way out of the force — and his new career began in earnest.

He headed immediately for a team in Iroquois Falls in Northern Ontario where he joined his brother Billy and the fabulous forward Aurel Joliat. But Ottawa Senators manager Tommy Gorman, who had just signed a hometown youngster named

King Clancy to a contract for $800, dangled a $1,200 pact in front of Boucher. Since Boucher and Clancy were great pals and the money was good, the slim centerman joined Ottawa.

Because Boucher didn't get enough playing time in Ottawa (he scored nine goals in 24 games), he was happy to join Frank Patrick's Vancouver Maroons of the Pacific Coast Hockey Association the following season. The Maroons owned his playing rights and had loaned him to the Senators for the 1921–22 season.

Apparently he couldn't have stayed in Ottawa if he'd wanted to. Frank and Lester Patrick insisted that because he had played two seasons in western Canada during his days as a Mountie, his playing rights belonged to the PCHA. They won their case and Boucher willingly joined Vancouver where he was promised more playing time. "I knew I'd not be freezing my buns as a bench-sitter in Ottawa," Boucher quipped.

In 1926, when the Patrick brothers sold the entire Western Hockey League (an amalgamation of the PCHA and the Western Canada Hockey League) to eastern clubs, Boucher was included in the Vancouver contingent purchased by the Boston Bruins.

But he never made it to Boston. Conn Smythe, a young Toronto coach, had been hired by Colonel John Hammond, president of the New York Rangers, an expansion club. Smythe's first assignment was to assemble a solid team. Smythe signed the Cook brothers, Bill and Bun, from Saskatoon, and asked them if there was a good centerman around who could fill out their line. They both said, "Get us Frankie Boucher." Smythe promptly purchased Boucher from Boston for $15,000 and almost fainted when Boucher made his appearance. He was pale and skinny, and his weight had dropped to 134 pounds. Over the summer, Boucher's wife, Ag, had almost died in childbirth, and the player had been under a great deal of stress.

"You're Boucher?" exclaimed Smythe. "Is this what I get for $15,000 — a bag of bones? Art Ross must be laughing his head off."

The Cook brothers told Smythe to "wait and see." Boucher would be well worth the $5,000 Smythe agreed to pay him.

The Cooks were right. Smythe's purchase of Boucher turned out to be one of the most satisfying deals in NHL history. The

Cooks and the former Mountie formed one of the greatest forward lines in history. In time, all three would be enshrined in the Hockey Hall of Fame.

The Cooks and Boucher arrived in New York a mere four days before the Rangers' opening game in 1926. After making a quick adjustment to the dizzying pace of life in Manhattan, they were ready for their opening game.

Buddy's Big Bonus

GNAT-SIZED Buddy O'Connor was feeling blue when the 1947–48 NHL season ended, and who could blame him? The diminutive Ranger center had led the league in scoring through most of the campaign, but in the final weekend he was nosed out for the Art Ross Trophy — by a single point. And it was former teammate Elmer Lach of the Canadiens who stole the title away from him — 61 points to 60.

O'Connor found consolation of sorts when he was named winner of both the Hart Trophy (MVP) and the Lady Byng Trophy (gentlemanly play). And he was overwhelmed when he added up his bonus — a small fortune at the time. The post-season payoff came in the following manner:

$500 — from the NHL for finishing second in the scoring race

$500 — from the Rangers as runner-up scorer

$1,000 — for winning the Hart Trophy (ahead of Frank Brimsek)

$1,000 — for winning the Lady Byng Trophy (ahead of Syl Apps)

$500 — for making the second All-Star team

$500 — share of Rangers' playoff money

Hockey's horn of plenty spilled the loot into O'Connor's lap after his seventh NHL season and his first as a Ranger. For half a dozen seasons, the 140-pounder had skated for the Canadiens, always in the shadow of first-team center Elmer Lach. He had burst on the scene as the pivot on the Habs' Razzle Dazzle Line, with linemates Gerry Heffernan and Pete Morin. The trio had been so hot in amateur ranks that the Canadiens signed them as a unit in 1941.

O'Connor was the only one who clicked in the NHL but it took a trade to New York in 1947 to ease him out of Elmer Lach's big shadow.

There was a note of irony in the deal. A few weeks before the trade was completed, the Habs and the Rangers engaged in a wild brawl. All of the players threw punches but it was O'Connor who suffered the most. The Rangers' Bryan Hextall threw a right that caught him in the face and broke his jaw. Guess what happened. When O'Connor joined the Rangers, his roommate turned out to be — Bryan Hextall.

The One that Got Away

THINK of it. The Rangers had Gordie Howe in camp for almost a week — and let him get away. How many Stanley Cups did that mistake cost them?

Growing up in Saskatoon, young Howe began his career as a goaltender. In 1942, in his first year in minor hockey, he was converted to defense and became the outstanding player on the King George Athletic Club team.

He moved on to bantam and midget hockey, and by the time he was 15 years old, he was heavily muscled, fast on his feet, and an accomplished stickhandler and shooter. He looked right at home whenever he played against older, tougher, more experienced players.

A Ranger scout spotted him in a game one day. "He's young but you've got to take a look at this kid," he told Frank Boucher, his general manager. "Why not invite him to training camp in Winnipeg?"

Howe was thrilled to receive the invitation but was thoroughly intimidated by the grown men with whom he shared ice time and dressing-room space.

The Ranger players, fighting for positions and contracts, paid little attention to him. They kidded him some. "First time away from home, kid? Got your homework with you?" And "Comin' to the bar with us tonight, Gord? Maybe we can buy you a milkshake." In the mess hall, one joker stole the food off his plate when he wasn't looking. The players suited up for a scrimmage and Gordie watched their every move. Some of the equipment he'd been handed was new to him. He'd never worn a jock before and watched curiously as the others pulled theirs on. Years later, at banquets, he would tell his audience that he almost put that jock on over his head.

In Winnipeg, Howe was homesick and terribly lonely. He missed his mother's home cooking and his friends. The Rangers suggested he try for a scholarship at Notre Dame College in Wilcox, Saskatchewan, a school with a fine hockey program. All Gordie wanted to do was go home.

The Rangers gave him train fare back to Saskatoon and wished him well. He'd been in Winnipeg less than a week.

Years later, when Howe was billed as the greatest player in the game and guiding Detroit to Stanley Cups, a Ranger scout would say, "It's too bad we didn't take a little more time with him in Winnipeg that fall. Why, he didn't even have a buddy from Saskatoon to room with, hardly a soul to talk to. Detroit manager Jack Adams learned a lesson from that. He took Gordie to Detroit's camp a year later and made sure four or five young kids from Saskatoon accompanied him. Not long after that, when Howe scored a couple of goals in an exhibition game, Adams signed him for $2,700 and the promise of a Red Wing jacket. And to think we could have had him . . ."

O'Connor, First Ranger MVP

OVER the years, several Rangers who in stature were little bigger than jockeys managed to carve out highly successful careers in the NHL. Camille Henry and Frank Boucher come readily to mind as skating Davids who stood up to the league's Goliaths. So does Buddy O'Connor, who stood five foot seven (standing on the tips of his toes) and weighed in at 140 pounds.

It takes courage and determination to battle for the puck against behemoths who tower over you and outweigh you by 50 or 60 pounds. O'Connor had both, and won more than his share of these skirmishes on skates. In the NHL, first with the Montreal Canadiens and then with the Rangers, the little man with the big bag of tricks showed the same finesse, the same wily moves that had made him a standout in amateur hockey — with the Montreal Royals of the Quebec Senior Hockey League. In that circuit, he centered a line that included wingers Pete Morin and Gerry Heffernan — a trio so flashy they were nicknamed the "Razzle Dazzle Line."

After six productive years with the Canadiens (1941–1947) and two Stanley Cup triumphs, O'Connor was traded to the Rangers. In 1947–48, he enjoyed his best NHL season, scoring 24 goals and adding 36 assists for 60 points. At season's end he was awarded both the Lady Byng Trophy for gentlemanly play and the coveted Hart Trophy as the NHL's most valuable player. His 60 points were one less than the total of Montreal's Elmer Lach, who captured the league's scoring championship. Later in the year, O'Connor received an unexpected third honor when he was named Canada's Athlete of the Year.

Finding room in the O'Connor household for several prestigious trophies proved to be no problem for the recipient. When his wife, Jennie, suggested they use the bowl of the Lady Byng

Lester Patrick replaced Conn Smythe as Ranger manager before the first game was played in 1926. — Bill Galloway

Defenseman Ivan "Ching" Johnston, a bald bouncer, was almost 30 when he joined the Rangers for their initial season. — Hockey Hall of Fame

One of the finest lines ever assembled. Left to right: Bill Cook, Frank Boucher, and Bun Cook, all honored members of the Hockey Hall of Fame. — Public Archives of Canada PA 50600

For a brief time goalie Lorne Chabot was renamed Chabotsky by Ranger publicists to attract more Jewish fans to games. — Hockey Hall of Fame

The Rangers' first home — Madison Square Garden. The rival New York Americans played the first professional game in New York on Garden ice in November 1925.
— New York Rangers

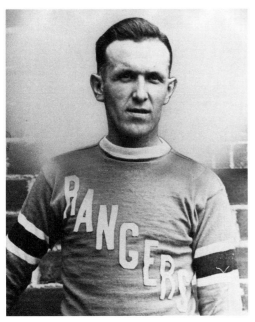

The Rangers' Frank Boucher won the Lady Byng Trophy a record seven times. Finally, the NHL allowed him to keep the original and ordered a replacement.
— Public Archives of Canada C 29494

The Rangers and the Canadiens fight during a game in 1935. The bench-clearing brawl required several of New York's finest to restore order. — Bill Galloway

Throughout the 1930s, Dave Kerr was one of the top goaltenders in hockey.

The 1937–38 Rangers. Back row, left to right: Lynn Patrick, Joe Cooper, Ott Heller, Art Coulter (captain), Lester Patrick (coach and manager), Frank Boucher, Neil Colville, Butch Keeling, Babe Pratt. Front row, left to right: Phil Watson, Bobby Kirk, Cecil Dillon, Dave Kerr, Clint Smith, Mac Colville, Bryan Hextall, Alex Shibicky, Harry Westerby (trainer).

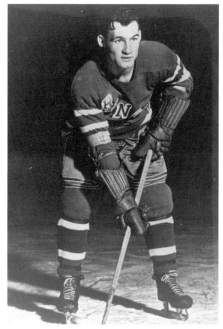

Mac Colville played on a line with his brother Neil and Alex Shibicky for several seasons.

Grant Warwick captured the Calder Trophy as Rookie of the Year in 1942.
— Bill Galloway

Phil Watson scored 127 goals in 546 games as a Ranger. He coached the club from 1955–56 through 1959.

In 1947–48, Buddy O'Connor won the Hart and Lady Byng Trophies — and was nosed out for the Art Ross Trophy by a single point.

Doug and Max Bentley played for the Rangers in 1953–54. — Hockey Hall of Fame

Goaltender Charlie Rayner won the Hart Trophy as league MVP in 1950.

Despite his slight frame, Camille "The Eel" Henry was an outstanding scorer and won the Calder Trophy in 1954.

Goalie Lorne "Gump" Worsley stopping "Boom Boom" Geoffrion. Worsley captured the Calder Trophy in 1953. — Hockey Hall of Fame

*Ranger tough guy "Leapin' Lou"
Fontinato in a familiar place —
the penalty box.*
— Hockey Hall of Fame

*One of the most popular
Rangers ever, Andy Bathgate
was inducted into the Hockey
Hall of Fame in 1987.*
— Hockey Hall of Fame

Trophy as a serving dish for vegetables, Buddy readily agreed. The gleaming bowl, filled with steaming carrots or cauliflower, was always an attention-getter, the first topic of conversation when friends sat down to dinner.

O'Connor's reputation for clean play is reflected in his career penalty stats — only 34 minutes in 509 games over 10 seasons. One might assume that must be some sort of NHL record. But Val Fonteyne, another former Ranger (who played for Detroit and Pittsburgh as well), broke even fewer rules. Fonteyne performed in 820 NHL games over 13 seasons and was penalized a total of 26 minutes.

He Should Have Been a Ranger

HERB Carnegie shuffles across the room and sits down at our table. He needs a little help with his chair because he's almost totally blind now.

Carnegie enjoys these monthly dinner dates with his old friends, most of them former NHLers, men like Harry Watson, Danny Lewicki, Cal Gardner, and Ed Litzenberger, to name a few. The former stars have just heard the good news — they'll all be getting some hefty checks as a result of winning the lawsuit against the league over surplus funds in the pension plan. When Carl Brewer walks in, he receives special attention and congratulations from those assembled. It was Brewer who initiated the suit against the league and helped win the $40 million owing.

There'll be no share of the dividend, no check for Herb Carnegie. He never played a game in the NHL, despite the fact he was one of the most highly skilled players of his era. There's the rub. His era was the late '40s and early '50s — when there was a color bar in the NHL — no blacks allowed. Toronto owner Conn Smythe was blunt about it. "I'd sign Carnegie in a minute," he told a reporter, "if I could turn him white." Smythe's racist comment didn't raise an eyebrow in the '40s.

Herb Carnegie should have been the first black player in the NHL and he should have been a Ranger. He was a better player than Willie O'Ree, who broke the race barrier in 1957 with the Boston Bruins. "No question Herb was a far better player than Willie," states Toronto columnist Robert Payne, "and O'Ree is my cousin."

For years Carnegie toiled in relative obscurity, a dominant force and perennial All-Star in the Quebec Senior Hockey League, a league that sent dozens of young players on to NHL stardom.

But not Carnegie. Not even after being named MVP for the third consecutive season. Neither Herb, his brother Ossie, nor Manny McIntyre — the only all-black line ever to play professional hockey — got the call to play in the NHL.

They did get to play one game at Madison Square Garden. In 1948–49, hockey's first all-black line played for Sherbrooke (Quebec) against the New York Rovers in a minor league attraction.

"Herb reminded me a lot of Stan Mikita," former NHL coach Joe Crozier once said. "We'd put him out when we were a man short and nobody could take the puck away from him."

The Rangers showed the most interest in Carnegie — after Jackie Robinson, who joined the Brooklyn Dodgers in 1947, proved that color lines could be shattered.

Carnegie recalls that Ranger coach Frank Boucher, in 1948, offered him a chance to play with New Haven, a Ranger farm club.

"I could have signed," sighs Carnegie. "But I was 29 by then and didn't think I'd be comfortable in New Haven. At that age, I thought my NHL chances were gone forever. As it turned out, later that season, two of New York's best centers, Edgar Laprade and Buddy O'Connor, were injured and were out of action for several weeks. If I'd been in New Haven, perhaps Frank Boucher would have called on me to replace one of them. Then I would have become the first black player in the NHL — not Willie O'Ree."

Sure, he has regrets. Who wouldn't? "I try not to think of

what might have been," he says. "I've had a great life in sports and I don't dwell on the past."

His career was not completely bereft of glory. Away from the rink, Carnegie excelled at golf and one year reigned as Canada's senior champion.

But hockey was his first love.

"My kids used to pore over my old scrapbooks and ask me if I was really as good as the clippings indicated," Herb laughs. "I found it hard to answer that."

A Present for the Ref

FORMER NHL referee Red Storey will never forget the compassion shown by a Ranger player during a game at Madison Square Garden one night. Nick Mickoski, a Ranger from 1948 through 1954, was tripped up by a Blackhawk. While falling, Mickoski's skate flew up and hit Storey in the crotch. Storey dropped like a stone, holding his midsection. He was whisked off the ice for medical attention. After a full examination of the bruised area, there was a further delay while someone mended the hole in his trousers. Then, sore but game, he grabbed his whistle and returned to duty.

When Storey returned to the ice, Mickoski immediately skated over to him. Storey anticipated a few words of sympathy. Instead, Mickoski stuck out his hand. In it was a gift.

"Red, I found something on the ice after they carried you off. I thought you might have lost them." With that, he opened his palm and offered Red a couple of jelly beans.

The Ranger Who Outplayed the Rocket

EVERY hockey fan knows the name Rocket Richard, the dynamic Montreal Canadien who once held the NHL record for goals with 544. But how many fans recall a Ranger winger named Pentti Lund, who finished his career with 500 fewer goals than Richard?

And yet, on at least one occasion, it was Lund who stole the limelight from Richard. It happened in the 1950 playoffs, Lund's second season in the NHL.

Lund was the first Finnish-born player to make his mark in the NHL. Born in Finland, he moved to Thunder Bay, Ontario, as a six-year-old and played all his minor hockey in Canada. In 1948–49, he clicked with the Rangers and captured the Calder Trophy as the NHL's top rookie after a 14–goal season. He improved to 18 goals the following season while Richard was scoring a league-leading 43 for Montreal. When the Rangers met the Habs in the 1950 semifinals, it was Lund's job to shadow the Rocket, the most explosive scorer in playoff history.

Richard was accustomed to being shadowed. Some checkers stuck to him like barnacles on a ship. But Lund took a different approach.

"I gave him a lot of room," he recalled. "But I always made sure I was there to cut him off every time he charged across the blue line. It seemed to work because he scored only one goal in the series which the Rangers won in five games. And the goal he scored was on a Montreal power play — when I was on the bench."

Lund's outstanding work against the Rocket earned him much praise from Ranger management. He was told he could count on a long career with the Blueshirts. But when his goal production fell to four the following season, New York traded him to Boston.

Dr. Tracy Casts His Spell

ELARLY in the 1950–51 NHL season, the Rangers needed someone like Dick Tracy to detect the reason for their 12-game winless streak. Instead, they got Dr. David Tracy, a hypnotist who claimed he could instill much-needed confidence in the players while they were in a trance-like state.

"Let's try it," said coach Frank Boucher. "Some of my boys are playing like they're already half asleep."

Prior to a game with Boston on November 15, the doctor stood in the center of the Ranger dressing room and soon had several players under his spell. One of the deepest sleepers was forward Tony Leswick. The good doctor delivered words of inspiration and encouragement and then snapped them awake.

When they charged out the door, eager to face the Bruins, one of the players said to Leswick, "What'd you think of all that?"

"Not much," said Leswick. "The guy didn't have any effect on me."

The Rangers performed well that night. They showed plenty of confidence and were tied with the Bruins (3–3) until the final minute. Then Boston scored a late goal to win the game 4–3.

Dr. Tracy was crushed. He said, "Next time I'll concentrate more on the Ranger goaltender, Charlie Rayner."

But he never got the chance. He was never invited back.

Ivan the Terrible

VERY Sunday morning, when a few old crocks get together for a hockey game in Pickering, Ontario, the play of defenseman Ivan Irwin, a 70-year-old wonder, draws a lot of comment.

"I can't get around the old bird," says Bobby Lalonde, who played in the NHL Theo Fleury–style for 11 seasons.

"And if you pass into the slot, the puck always seems to hit one of his big boots," states Carl Brewer.

"And he's always laughing out there, always happy to see one of us mess up," says Bo Elik, another former pro.

Irwin, nicknamed Ivan the Terrible when he played for the Rangers in the early 1950s, hasn't lost his knack for playing positional hockey. "When you have one of the weakest shots in the NHL and you can't skate, you have to know how to play positionally," he once told a reporter.

When asked about his offensive play as a Ranger, his booming laugh preceded his answer. "I scored just two goals in my NHL career, and wouldn't you know, when they held a surprise 65th birthday party for me a few years ago, someone found a film of one of them. That must have been like looking for a needle in a haystack."

Ivan Irwin is remembered for two reasons (no, not his pair of goals) — he was the first NHLer to cut the palms out of his gloves. That made it easier for him to grab an opponent by the shirt and escape a penalty because the referee couldn't detect the grab.

"He's also remembered," says former referee Red Storey, "because he was the best fighter I ever saw in hockey. I never saw him lose a fight in the NHL or any other league. He has the biggest hands I've ever seen."

Storey recalls a fight between Irwin and a player named Dean McBride that erupted during a minor league game played in Quebec City almost fifty years ago. When McBride swung his stick at Irwin, cutting his lip clean through, the gloves came off.

The two players slammed into each other and exchanged sledge-hammer blows. The battle raged on and on. Five minutes, six, then eight, then 10, and still they slugged it out. Finally, McBride went down and couldn't get up. Irwin fell on top of him. Both men were totally exhausted. McBride's face was a mass of welts, cuts, and bruises, while Irwin bled from a torn lip and a gashed ear.

Irwin told me recently, "I've been in a few scraps in my career but I'll never forget that battle with McBride. When it was over, we were both so tired and beat up we could hardly skate to the penalty box."

So Long, Arthur

THE 1991–92 NHL season began at Madison Square Garden with a familiar face missing from rinkside. Arthur Reichert, who figured in more goals than any man in history, retired after six decades of goal judging and timing of NHL games. Reichert's nimble finger (or was it his thumb?) triggered thousands of red lights over the years — he started in 1932 — and when asked to select his most famous goal, he selected three.

"I was on duty the night Bill Mosienko of Chicago fired three goals in 21 seconds and I got to signal them," he recalls. "The date was March 23, 1952, and Mosienko just missed a fourth goal on the same shift. It was the last game of the season."

Another game Reichert recalls with far less enthusiasm was the one in which Ranger coach Emile Francis circled the rink to argue with him about a disputed goal. Francis was then attacked by some rowdy fans and Reichert decided to scurry to safety until the donnybrook was over.

Ranger Star Introduces Slapshot

WHO invented hockey's slapshot? Was it Boom Boom Geoffrion, Bobby Hull, Stan Mikita, or Andy Bathgate? Over the years, all four have been credited with introducing the slapper to hockey.

But a good 15 years before any of the above made it to the NHL, a couple of New York Rangers were experimenting with slapshots in scrimmage sessions, and when one of them began using it in games, the results were impressive.

Winger Alex Shibicky joined New York in 1935–36 and was surprised to see teammate Bun Cook uncorking the occasional slapshot during Ranger practices. Cook even used it once in an exhibition game. Shibicky, a four-goal scorer that season, was fascinated with the new shot and quickly mastered it.

Cook was hesitant about using the new shot in a big league game, but Shibicky had no reservations. He started slapping the puck whenever the occasion warranted it.

"I was the leading goal scorer in New York and I always credited the slapshot for that," he would say in retirement. "Got 24 goals one season and a lot of them came off the slapper."

Shibicky seldom raised the stick above his waist when unloading his slapshot. "I'd hit the ice about two inches behind the puck and really follow through on the shot. That's the secret to a good slapshot. When you get a good one away, it's a beautiful sight to see."

He'd simply shaken his head when he heard people credit Bobby Hull and Boom Boom Geoffrion for the creation of the slapshot. "What a bunch of malarkey that is," he would say.

Shibicky was a key member of New York's Stanley Cup–winning team in 1940. He played in the final series against Toronto despite the fact he'd suffered a broken right ankle. The injury kept him out of one game — only because the ankle was so swollen he couldn't get his skate boot on. A shoemaker produced a special boot for the next contest, the club doctors supplied some painkillers, and Shibicky played a solid game, even though he had difficulty turning to his right.

Years later, in the 1964 finals, defenseman Bobby Baun of the Leafs would gain everlasting fame for scoring a winning goal in overtime while skating on a broken ankle. But Baun's moment of glory took place before millions watching on television. By then, Shibicky's gutsy effort, like his introduction of the slapshot, was all but forgotten.

Worsley Drinks Coach under the Table

GOALTENDER Gump Worsley and Ranger coach Phil Watson had more blowups and exchanged more insults than Ralph and Alice Cramden. Put simply, they couldn't stand each other. Gump once said of Watson, "That little bastard made me so mad, I was ready to choke him."

Worsley was Watson's favorite whipping boy. He constantly badgered him about everything from his work ethic to his waistline. One year, the Rangers and the Black Hawks played exhibition games in Europe. Before a game in France, Watson told reporters, "That Worsley's drunk so much wine, when he stops the puck with his belly pad tonight, the burgundy's going to spurt right out his ears."

Another time, enraged when Worsley gave up a pair of soft goals one night, Watson sneered, "You can't play goal in the NHL with a big beer belly getting in your way." Worsley uttered a classic retort. "You tell Watson," he said, "I don't drink beer. I've always been a VO [rye] drinker."

Worsley established his reputation as a drinking man during his first training camp with the Rangers in 1952–53. And Watson helped him do it.

Watson challenged the rookie. "You think you're a hotshot drinker. I can drink you under the table any day." He called for a bottle and some glasses. The coach and the rookie, with the rest of the players forming a cheering section, faced off across the table. The glasses were filled and emptied, filled and emptied again. Another bottle replaced the first and the contest continued.

Finally, Watson's eyes turned glassy. He slumped back in his chair and almost slid to the floor. Worsley belched, lurched to his feet, and received a chorus of cheers from his mates.

Tracking Down Camille

CAMILLE (the Eel) Henry was a will-o'-the-wisp goalscorer for the Rangers in the '50s, a skinny little guy (five foot six, 140 pounds) whose knack for tip-in goals and power-play scores bordered on the phenomenal. He scored 24 goals for the Rangers in 1953–54, his rookie season, and won the Calder Trophy over more publicized performers like Earl Reibel and Jean Beliveau.

"I never weighed more than 137 pounds," he once said, "but the coaches and trainers would never let the reporters see me get on the scales. They added 20 pounds whenever they gave the figures out."

He invested his money in real estate and once owned three houses. He married a famous Quebec singer and was envied and admired for the way he lived his life.

What wasn't generally known was that Henry was a problem drinker — not on game days, perhaps — but a slave to the bottle nevertheless. He came by his addiction honestly for his father and his grandfather were both alcoholics.

In 1994, writer Michael Ulmer, on assignment for the *Hockey News*, traced Henry to the town of Charlesbourg, Quebec, where the former hockey star declared himself to be a recovering alcoholic (seven years on the wagon) but suffering from diabetes, epilepsy, and chronic back pain. He recited a list of old hockey injuries that makes one shudder: two broken arms, several severe concussions, torn ligaments in both knees, a faceful of scars, and an aching back that required a spinal fusion.

His second marriage ended years ago, so Henry lives alone, a recluse. He blames no one but himself for his problems and is thankful to the NHL's emergency assistance fund for providing him with $5,000 a year to cover insulin costs. His NHL pension of $7,000 barely covers his rent and day-to-day living costs. He told Ulmer he had a little more than $300 in the bank, that he never earned more than $9,000 a year since leaving hockey, and that he depends on $20 to get through each week.

There was some good news for Henry in 1996. Thanks to court action initiated by Carl Brewer, a former opponent, the settlement of a dispute between former NHL players and the league over $40–50 million in surplus pension funds resulted in a share to Henry of about $86,000. That windfall and the fact he'll soon be eligible for the old age pension makes him feel like a millionaire.

For comparison's sake, Ulmer found that an NHLer who played in 400 games and retired after the 1986–87 season, aside from any monies from the settlement mentioned above, is eligible for a pension of $250,000 at the age of 55.

The Bentleys' Last Hurrah

IT was past mid-season in 1954 when the Rangers placed a call for help. Would Doug Bentley, brother to the Rangers' Max, come out of retirement and assist the club in a long-shot bid for the playoffs? Doug would and did. He arrived in New York in time for a game with Boston. Despite the fact he'd been away from hockey for two seasons, Doug scored a goal and added three assists. Brother Max had two goals and two assists. At 38 (four years older than Max), Doug played in 20 games to finish out the season. The Bentley brothers failed (by four points) to push the Rangers into the 1954 playoffs. They retired after that season with one slim point separating their career totals: Max had 544, Doug 543.

THE MUZZ PATRICK ERA

Gadsby Survives Tragedy at Sea

THE Canada-bound steamship *Athenia* was off the Irish coast when the German torpedo struck with devastating force. It was shortly after the outbreak of the Second World War and the Nazi submarine was waiting for the ship — the last passenger liner to leave Southampton.

Twelve-year-old Bill Gadsby, traveling with his mother, was knocked out of his bunk by the explosion which ripped a huge hole in the hull and quickly sent the liner to the bottom of the sea. The Gadsbys — and about 50 other passengers — found themselves jammed into a single lifeboat. Young Bill remembers it being pitch dark and very cold. "I was too young to realize how serious the situation was," he says. "But I saw men and women going crazy with panic. I saw up close the horror, the terrible things I can never forget."

Within hours the lifeboat was spotted by a rescue ship and the survivors returned to Southampton. The Gadsbys finally arrived home via New York on the *Mauretania*. When the ship docked, Gadsby no doubt stared goggle-eyed at the towering skyscrapers of Manhattan, never dreaming that one day he would return to New York and walk among the tall buildings, and play hockey at Madison Square Garden.

He turned pro at 18 with the Chicago Black Hawks organization and played two seasons of junior hockey with Edmonton. After 12 games at Kansas City in 1946–47 — as a left winger — he was called up to the Hawks, was shifted to defense, and never played forward again. In 1952, he contracted polio and was placed in isolation for 10 days. In that era, before Dr. Jonas Salk invented his miraculous vaccine, polio crippled thousands of young people. Gadsby was fortunate, for his symptoms gradually disappeared. He was with Chicago until the 1954–55 season, when he was traded to the Rangers with Pete Conacher in return for Nick Mickoski and Allan Stanley.

The reason behind Gadsby's departure from Chicago is a simple one. The previous season Chicago had played Detroit in Omaha, Nebraska. The Black Hawks attendance had been pitiful and playing a game in Omaha seemed like a good idea at the time. During the game, Gadsby and Detroit Coach Tommy Ivan got into a shouting match and Gadsby called the dapper Ivan every name in the book. That summer Ivan was hired as general manager of the Hawks and Gadsby knew he was toast.

He was reluctant at first to join the Rangers, but Frank Boucher urged him to give New York a chance. He did, and quickly became a fan favorite with his reckless, fearless style of play.

He blossomed with the Rangers and made the first All-Star team three times, in 1956, 1958, and 1959. He set a record for defensemen with 46 assists in the 1958–59 season, breaking Doug Harvey's mark of 44 established two years earlier.

In 1960, Gadsby and Eddie Shack were traded to Detroit in return for Red Kelly and Billy McNeill. When the trade was announced, the Rangers were in Detroit and Shack was overjoyed. "What a relief to get away from the Rangers," he announced. Gadsby wisely said nothing. Within hours the trade was canceled. Red Kelly had refused to report to New York and announced his retirement. Later he would be shipped to Toronto where he would lead the Leafs to four Stanley Cups. Shack and Gadsby returned to the Rangers, Shack no doubt saying, "What a relief it is to be back."

Gadsby was traded to Detroit the following season and wound up playing 20 years in the NHL but never on a Stanley Cup winner.

His penchant for getting in the path of a puck or a stick was a costly one. His nose was broken seven times. His face bears the scars from over 400 stitches. His left leg was broken twice and both his big toes and his thumbs have been fractured.

After his playing days, he turned to coaching. His stint as coach of the Red Wings was remarkably brief. He survived one season (1968–69) with a poor club and won his first two games the following year. Team owner Bruce Norris congratulated him on his fine work after the second victory. The next afternoon, Norris fired him. "I decided to make a change," Norris explained. Gadsby took his hurts, his firing, all his disappointments in stride. He survived two decades at the top of his profession and in 1970, he became an honored member of hockey's Hall of Fame. Not bad for a kid who might have been crippled with polio or gone down with the *Athenia*.

Shack: A Memorable Ranger Character

WHEN Eddie Shack joined the New York Rangers in 1958, Toronto sportswriter Milt Dunnell wrote that he "landed in New York as silently as a tornado." His undisciplined play caused general manager Muzz Patrick to say, "I'd pay two bucks anytime to watch him skate but I wouldn't pay a dime to watch him play hockey."

Shack was a crowd favorite, a flashy skater and unpredictable playmaker with a booming shot. He became known as the Entertainer. He loved to hit and was as likely to steamroll over a teammate as an opponent. Shack had little schooling, but he soon learned the word "holdout," and became one, despite the fact he'd scored a modest eight goals the season before. And he clashed with coach Phil Watson almost from his first day on the job. Once, when Watson delivered a blistering lecture to his players, he turned to Shack and said, "What do you think of that, Shack?" Eddie put a finger to his ear, went "phffft, phffft" as if to say the talk went in one ear and out the other. It cracked the players up. Shack could neither read nor write, but he was street-smart and parlayed his hockey ability, during and after his career, into business deals that netted him a small fortune. He didn't stay long with one team because he drove coaches nutty. But give him credit. He played for 17 seasons with six different clubs and scored 239 goals.

Bobby Hull a Ranger? You're Kidding!

IT really happened. Bobby Hull once scored 14 goals while skating in a Ranger uniform. In the spring of 1959, following Hull's sophmore season as a Chicago Blackhawk, the Rangers embarked on a tour of Europe with the Boston Bruins. Ranger management recruited Hull for the series of exhibition games, and the youngster produced 14 goals during the 23-game tour. The players received $1,000 each for their participation.

It was during this tour that Hull learned to pace himself and not chase all over the ice after the puck. The following season he vaulted to the top of the NHL scoring parade with 81 points. But by then, of course, he was back wearing a Chicago uniform.

A Race to the Wire

OLDTIME Ranger fans will recall the crushing disappointment that came with the end of the 1958–59 NHL season. New York and Toronto were engaged in a battle for the fourth and final playoff position. Punch Imlach, in his rookie season as the Leafs' whipcracker coach, lashed his club from last place to a virtual tie with the Rangers on the final weekend of the season. Earlier, Ranger coach Phil Watson had boasted, "I've known Imlach a long time and I don't like the guy. I'll tell you one thing. He's not going to put my team out of the playoffs. I'm going to put his team out of the playoffs."

But on the final night of the regular season, Watson's Rangers were humbled 4–2 by Montreal while Imlach's Leafs, after falling behind 2–0 to Detroit, rallied for a 6–4 triumph. The Leafs were in, the Rangers out, sidelined by a single point. Phil Watson couldn't decide whether to jump off the Brooklyn Bridge or the George Washington Bridge.

There were howls of anger along Broadway, and goaltender Gump Worsley was fingered as the player who'd cost the Rangers an almost certain playoff berth. Worsley was rather porous in the stretch, allowing 32 goals in his team's final 7 games when the Rangers lost six of seven games.

But another finger might have been pointed at the Rangers' boss man, General John Reed Kilpatrick. Late in the season he made a decision that may have cost the New Yorkers a chance to grab the Stanley Cup.

New York played in Boston one night and were beaten by the Bruins in a close game. After the match, Phil Watson checked the rules and discovered the Bruins had used an ineligible player in the game. "We should protest the match," he told his employers. "I'm sure the league will back us up and award us the two points we lost to the Bruins."

But General John Reed Kilpatrick would not hear of it. "The

Rangers don't operate like that," he told Watson. "We must act like gentlemen."

Later, when it became clear that the two lost points would have enabled the Rangers to edge Imlach's Leafs by a single point and gain a playoff berth, Kilpatrick had little to say while Watson could only snort, "Gentlemen. That's the last thing I ever want anybody to call my team."

Watson's Postgame Punishment

A coach couldn't get away with it today. The NHLPA wouldn't allow it.

But back in the '50s, coach Phil Watson ruled the Ranger roost. When he barked, "Jump!" his players almost banged their heads on the ceiling. One night he ordered them on the ice for a full-scale practice immediately after a game. That was an NHL "first."

On a February night in 1959, Ranger goalie Gump Worsley was en route to a shutout victory over the best team in hockey, the Montreal Canadiens. Midway through the third period, the Rangers were leading 1–0. Then the Habs (winners of three straight Stanley Cups and waltzing towards a fourth) suddenly exploded for five straight goals. Three of them came in four minutes as they scuttled New York 5–1.

The shell-shocked Rangers stumbled into their dressing room after the shellacking and began hurling gloves, sticks, and jerseys against the walls. They were stunned when a red-faced Phil Watson stormed into their ranks and screamed like a drill sergeant, "You're all going to pay for this. Put that equipment back on!"

He ordered the sullen players back on the ice for a grueling practice. The players weren't the only ones in shock. Their wives phoned their babysitters to say, "We'll be a lot later than we expected."

Gump Worsley was the only Ranger to be excused from the midnight workout and he remembers it well.

"When Watson said that I was excused, I got dressed as fast as I could and took off. But I didn't go home. I sat far up in the seats out of Watson's sight. I watched him put my teammates through drill after drill for at least an hour. What a bastard! It was painful to watch, punishment like I'd never seen before — a terrible thing."

Andy Bathgate Speaks Out

I N December 1959, Andy Bathgate, star right winger with the New York Rangers, spoke out against unnecessary violence in the NHL — and got his knuckles rapped.

In an article for *True* magazine, Bathgate predicted, "There will be a death on the ice any day now." With an assist from writer Dave Anderson, Bathgate decided to write about and condemn "spearing" or stabbing an opponent with the blade of the stick.

This followed an ugly incident in which Montreal's Doug Harvey (who later said he did it on purpose) speared New York's Red Sullivan right in front of the Ranger bench. Sullivan suffered a ruptured spleen and nearly died from the blow to his mid-section.

Bathgate also targeted the Bruins' Fern Flaman. "The guys who spear make sure the referee isn't looking — as Boston's Fernie Flaman did when he almost poked my eye out with his stick blade," he wrote.

Flaman denied the charge, stating that he'd lost his balance and the hit on Bathgate was accidental.

"I don't consider it accidental," Bathgate declared. "He's been involved in too many 'accidents' so why should anyone believe him now."

Walter Brown, president of the Bruins, was incensed over the Bathgate article. "I've had Flaman since he was 15 years old and there isn't a mean bone in his body. Who else did Bathgate finger?"

He was told that Bathgate had compiled a list of the NHL's spear carriers. The accused included Ted Lindsay (Black Hawks); Tom Johnson and Doug Harvey (Montreal); Gordie Howe (Detroit); Flaman; and even a Ranger teammate, Lou Fontinato.

NHL president Clarence Campbell levied a $1,000 fine against Bathgate for his controversial remarks. Ghostwriter Anderson was barred from the Ranger locker room for several weeks.

Before the next season rolled around, the NHL defined spearing as a five-minute major penalty as well as a game misconduct, thus indicating that Bathgate's criticism was entirely justified.

Bathgate played 10 years on Broadway as one of the NHL's premier right wings. He captured the Hart Trophy as league MVP in 1959. Ranger fans often argue over who was the greatest — Bathgate or Rod Gilbert?

"Andy Bathgate was the best by far," states former teammate and Hall-of-Famer Harry Howell. "He was our star, our premier player, our marquee attraction, and deservedly so."

Bathgate's stats as a Ranger are impressive. He scored 729 points in 719 games, an average of 1.01 points per game. Gilbert tallied 406 goals and 1,021 points in 1,065 games for an average of .95 per game.

For an opinion from a non-Ranger, we sought out Hall-of-Fame goaltender Glenn Hall. Hall said, "I rank him in the top 20 of all time. He was that great."

Belisle Was Just Following Orders

ANNY Belisle never took himself — or the game of hockey — too seriously.

In 1960, Danny received the greatest Christmas gift he would ever get — a chance to play for the New York Rangers on Christmas Day. His NHL debut would be against the Montreal Canadiens, who were seeking a sixth consecutive Stanley Cup title.

The Rangers, deep in the league basement, had lost some key players to injuries — Dean Prentice and Camille Henry to name a couple — and Belisle was called up from Vancouver to replace Henry in the lineup. The rookie responded with a goal in his first NHL game and scored another in the three games that followed. Not bad, he said to himself, beginning to think he'd stick around for awhile.

In the Ranger dressing room before the next game, Belisle was putting the last of his equipment in place when coach Alf Pike stuck his head in the door and said, "Hey, kid. Not so fast. Camille Henry may be fit enough to play tonight. Take your gear off."

Belisle shrugged and started to strip off his equipment. Two minutes later, Pike was back with further instructions. "Hey, kid, you better suit up. Henry probably can't play, after all." So Belisle started to haul his equipment back on.

Moments later, Pike made a third appearance. "Hey, kid, Henry's still a question mark but he's feeling better. Tell you what . . . get half-dressed."

By this time, Belisle had had enough. But in those days, rookies didn't dare voice an opinion. Dutifully, he pulled on his shin pads and socks and stepped into his hockey pants. Then he put on his street shoes and laced them up. He donned his shirt and knotted his tie. He was half-dressed. Then he sat back and waited.

The other Rangers, when they looked at him, started to break up. Belisle began to chuckle too. Soon howls of laughter filled the dressing room.

Outside the door, Pike heard the commotion and stuck his head in the door.

"What the hell is going on in here?" he barked. Then he saw Belisle. "Christ!" he said, "Take your goddamn gear off, Belisle, and turn it in. Henry will play tonight if it kills him."

"And that was my last game in the NHL," laughs Belisle. "I did exactly what the coach ordered — I got half-dressed. But putting on that shirt and tie pissed him off so much I was back in the minors the following day."

Bathgate's Ross Trophy Chances Scuttled in '62

F ROM the mid-fifties through the mid-sixties, Andy Bathgate was one of the NHL's most prolific scorers. Yet he never captured the Art Ross Trophy as the league's individual scoring leader.

He did come close, finishing fourth four times, third twice, and second three times.

His best chance to win the scoring honors came in 1962 when he led Chicago's Bobby Hull by a single point after 69 games. The final game in New York featured a Bathgate-Hull confrontation with Hull striving to overtake Bathgate, to win the scoring crown, and to score 50 goals for the first time in his career.

The Golden Jet scored his 50th early in the game (tying Rocket Richard and Boom Boom Geoffrion as hockey's only 50-goal scorers) and logged over 30 minutes of ice time in his attempt to get 51.

With less than a minute to play, and the Rangers trailing by three goals, Bathgate and Hull each had 84 points. But Hull had

50 goals to Bathgate's 28, and it was common knowledge the Ross Trophy would go to the player with the most goals in the event of a tie.

Bathgate skated out, determined to get a point. At least he hoped to get one final shot on net. The Hawks were just as determined to keep him off the scoresheet.

Bobby Hull, on the Chicago bench, turned to coach Rudy Pilous, "Let me go out and check him."

"Siddown," growled Pilous. "Reggie Fleming's the perfect guy for that job."

Fleming, one of the toughest, crudest men in hockey, hopped the boards and lined up opposite Bathgate. The puck was dropped. Bathgate lunged for it and Fleming lunged for Bathgate. He grabbed his stick and jumped on his back. Bathgate went down to his knees as another Ranger scooted away with the puck. The referee's arm shot up. Delayed penalty. Fleming was busy breaking a number of rules.

Meanwhile, the Rangers moved the puck from man to man, waiting for Bathgate to get up. The seconds ticked away. The referee's arm stayed up. He'd blow his whistle when the Hawks touched the puck. In front of him, Fleming continued to wrestle with Bathgate — clutching, holding, punching, pushing.

The Rangers wanted a whistle. One of them shoveled the puck towards a Black Hawk. He jumped aside and refused to touch it. Still no whistle. More seconds ticked off the clock. The crowd was in an uproar. Bathgate continued to struggle under the weight of Fleming.

The second hand reached the top of the clock and the game was over. The crowd howled its indignation.

On the ice, a weary Bathgate struggled to his feet, his chance to be scoring champ gone forever. He would not come so close again.

On the Hawk bench, players pounded a grinning Hull on the back. Then they pummeled Fleming on the gloves and back, congratulating him on his masterful wrestling display, one that went unpunished, one that assured his teammate of a scoring crown.

Big Goals from Bathgate

THE Rangers met the Red Wings with much at stake on March 14, 1962. The teams were tied in points for the final play-off berth and both teams needed a victory. The game started poorly for New York. Detroit's Gordie Howe scored a picture goal in the second period — his 500th career marker — to earn a standing ovation. It took a third period tie-breaking goal by Andy Bathgate to trigger a much louder ovation than the one Howe received.

However, it was a goal that Bathgate should not have been allowed to score. It came on a penalty shot — one that should have been awarded to Ranger teammate Dean Prentice. When Prentice broke in alone, Red Wing goalie Hank Bassen threw his stick at the puck, spoiling any chance Prentice had to score. Referee Eddie Powers, for some reason, awarded the free shot to Bathgate, New York's top scorer. Moments later, Bathgate backhanded the puck past Bassen for what proved to be the winning goal. The goal sparked the Rangers to a 3-1-1 record in the next two weeks and a playoff berth over the Red Wings by a margin of four points. A few months later, in games from December 1962, to January 5, 1963, Andy Bathgate set a "modern-day" NHL record by scoring in 10 consecutive games. He established the mark by scoring twice in a game at Montreal (11 goals in 10 games) to give the Rangers a 2–2 tie. The current record holder is Charlie Simmer of the Kings who scored in 13 consecutive games in 1979–80.

Jennings's Hall Induction Angers Columnist

"TODAY the game of hockey lost one of its greatest friends and contributors," said NHL president Clarence Campbell on August 17, 1981. "Bill Jennings's intellect, common sense, and vision contributed greatly to the NHL's growth from six to 21 teams. His dedication to the game and to the NHL is legendary; his dedication to the New York Rangers is unparalleled."

Earlier that day, Jennings, 61, the most powerful governor in the NHL, had lost an endurance battle with cancer. Since 1962, he had served as president of the New York Rangers, a non-paying position.

Ten years before his death, the gray-haired graduate of Princeton and Yale law schools, a hockey visionary, had made the following points:

1. **Canada's largest non-NHL cities — Ottawa, Winnipeg, Edmonton, Calgary, and Quebec — are too small to support major-league hockey.**
2. **Hockey will someday surpass football, baseball, and basketball in popularity among American sports fans.**
3. **Canadian and American college hockey associations should adopt professional rules.**
4. **Hockey will boom in the southern states.**
5. **The NHL will add a six-team European Division within 10 years.**
6. **The NHL should make greater use of the penalty shot.**

Jennings took a slap at then referee-in-chief Ian "Scotty" Morrison by stating, "As for more penalty shots, first we have to get a referee-in-chief who believes in them."

Jennings served as chairman of the League's Board of Governors from 1968 to 1970 and was the main architect of the expansion of the NHL from six to 18 cities in the '70s.

In 1966, Jennings originated the Lester Patrick Award, which annually honors persons for outstanding service to hockey in the United States. He captured the award in 1971. He was elected to the Hockey Hall of Fame in 1976 and the United States Hockey Hall of Fame in 1981. While many applauded this rare double honor, his induction to the hockey hall in Toronto was lambasted by veteran Canadian sports columnist Jim Coleman.

Coleman wrote: "Let's have Three Rousing Cheers for good old Bill Jennings, who brought us those wildly exciting hockey teams: the Washington Capitals, Kansas City Scouts, and California Seals . . . Bless you, Billy boy; we're all sobbing with gratitude."

———

Note: In 1976, the Caps, the Scouts, and the Seals were three of the NHL's most pathetic teams. The Caps finished 11-59-10, the Scouts were 12-56-12, and the Seals were 27-42-11.

Leapin' Lou Doesn't Dwell on the Past

RUGGED defenseman Lou Fontinato — "Leapin Lou" to a few million fans — was one of the most colorful Rangers ever. His Madison Square Garden supporters admired his bashing style, his fearless, rhino-like charges that stunned opponents large and small. Fans hated him everywhere else around the league.

Today he lives alone on his cattle farm near Guelph, Ontario. He'll gladly talk about tractors and cattle and mending fences. A typical farmer, he goes to bed at sundown and rises before dawn. He seldom talks hockey, doesn't dwell on the headlines he helped create during his turbulent stay in the NHL — first as a Ranger, then as a Canadien. It doesn't matter to him if fans have forgotten he started his career as a replacement for Allan Stanley and that he ended it with a near-fatal injury.

If he's remembered at all after almost 35 years away from the NHL stage, it's mainly for a few seconds of devil-may-care behavior when he duked it out with Gordie Howe and led with his nose. When the brief battle ended, a reporter would describe Fontinato's battered nose as "an afterthought, like it was stuck on his weatherbeaten face by a careless sculptor."

It was muscular Howe, with biceps and shoulders like Schwarzenegger, who filled the role of Fontinato's personal nose sculptor. It began when Eddie Shack, a Ranger teammate, went after Howe in New York one night, nipping at his heels like a yappy dog, tormenting the big man in the Red Wing uniform until his blood began to boil. The gloves flew off behind the Ranger net where Howe planned to administer a solid punch to Shack's prominent nose. But it was another beak that would take the full force of the blow.

Fontinato raced to the scene, pushed Shack aside, and leaped at Howe. "I threw everything at him," he would later recall, "and nothin' happened. The best punch I ever threw didn't even faze the guy. He didn't seem to notice it. Geez, I said to myself, why doesn't the guy go down? Then pow! Gordie hit me with a dandy punch. Just a short one, mind you — but it caught me right in the nose and spread it all over my face. Broke all the blood vessels and everything."

An alert photographer captured the damage on film, and photos of Fontinato's shattered proboscis appeared in papers from coast to coast.

Today, Fontinato would rather talk about a new calf, the cost of feed, or the weather than about his nine-year career in the NHL, which ended abruptly when he suffered a broken neck in a game at the Montreal Forum during the 1962–63 season.

As for the Howe incident, there's not much he has to say about that either. "It doesn't interest me," Fontinato states with a shrug. "But other people always want to hear about it."

Leaving Rangers a Break for Gump

FOR 10 NHL seasons, Lorne "Gump" Worsley was the netminder for various Ranger lineups that were often dreadfully inept. Gump and his teammates seldom made the playoffs and when they did, they were tossed aside like yesterday's newspaper. A regular night's work for Gump would be one in which he faced about 50 shots. A renowned quipster, Gump was asked one day to name the team that gave him the most trouble. "The Rangers," he replied without hesitation. It made all the papers.

After the 1963 season, on the eve of the annual draft meetings, Gump was barhopping with his boss, Ranger general manager Muzz Patrick. Gump had heard some disturbing rumors about his future, so he bluntly asked, "Muzz, you gonna trade me?"

"Of course not," was the answer. "How would we ever replace you in New York?"

"If you do trade me," Gump continued. "Deal me to Montreal. This would be hockey heaven for a guy like me."

"We're not gonna trade you, Gump."

The next day, Muzz Patrick traded Worsley to Montreal and it turned his career around. He played most of six seasons for the Habs, no longer peppered by 50 or more shots per game. He went from obscurity to stardom and backstopped his team to four Stanley Cups.

Asked to comment on the difference between playing for the two teams, Gump said, "In New York we wanted to win the games. In Montreal we had to win the games. Simple as that."

Gump was motivated to do his best as a Hab because legendary goalie Jacques Plante went to the Rangers in the trade.

"I had to prove to the Montreal fans that I was just as good as Plante, didn't I? And I think I did that before very long."

Gump has encountered plenty of heroes and villains in his

time. He talked about some of his good times — and bad — on the eve of his induction into the Hockey Hall of Fame in 1980.

"I was with the Rangers, playing against Gordie Howe one night. In a goalmouth scramble, I fell on my back while the puck popped high in the air. It came down and landed squarely on my face. And who do I see lookin' down at me, his stick poised for a rebound? Yeah, big Gordie Howe.

"He could have torn my kisser apart if he'd shot," said Gump. "I closed my eyes and gritted my teeth. When I looked up again, he'd eased the puck off my face and tucked it underneath me while the ref blew the play dead. Funny how you don't forget things like that."

And the bad?

"Guys like Reggie Jackson, the ball player. My son Dean asked him for an autograph once in a restaurant. Jackson wasn't eating or anything and the kid was polite. Said 'Excuse me,' and 'Please.' Jackson said, 'No,' and turned away. Just like that. 'No.'

"I guess I had it all wrong when I played. I always thought that signing autographs, especially when a kid asked politely, was part of the job."

Any other unpleasant memories?

"Yeah, my fear of flying. I hated planes. I was on a flight once when there was so much turbulence the meals jumped off the trays and stained our clothes. A flight attendant came by and promised that the airline would pay for the cleaning of all jackets and slacks. I said, 'That's great. What about my shorts?'"

By the time he was closing in on 40, he'd pretty well decided he'd had enough hockey. Besides, the Habs had a tall kid named Dryden who was looking pretty good.

But the Minnesota North Stars came calling, offered Sam Pollock some money for Gump's services, then offered Gump a lot more money than he ever thought he'd make in hockey. So he stayed in the league another four seasons, his career spanning 21 seasons in all.

THE EMILE FRANCIS ERA

Francis Waded In — and
Wound Up in Court

T ODAY, former Ranger coach Emile Francis can laugh about his most embarrassing moment in hockey. But when it happened — a bizarre and shocking spectacle that began with a goal judge's tardy finger and wound up in court — it was a serious and costly business.

The Rangers were leading Detroit 2–1 late in a game at Madison Square Garden. Suddenly, the Wings' Norm Ullman squirted through the New York defense, went in on goal, and scored to tie the game.

Or did he? Arthur Reichert, the goal judge, failed to trigger the red light signaling a score for several seconds. Perhaps he wanted to make sure the puck was fully over the goal line. When Reichert did jab his finger on the button and the bulb turned crimson, so did Francis.

Francis darted away from the Ranger bench, dashed around ushers and ice cream vendors, and made a beeline to where the goal judge sat. In a loud voice, he berated the astonished official and demanded to know why he'd procrastinated so long before signaling a score. "I know why, you jackass. Because you didn't see the puck go in," he screamed.

A fan sitting nearby objected to the tirade and told Francis to shut up and get lost. "Leave the poor guy alone," he bellowed. He started to rise from his seat and Francis, now thoroughly enraged, belted the spectator.

But the mouthy fan wasn't alone. Two of his pals surged forward and began to lay a beating on the diminutive coach. A roundhouse punch landed squarely on Francis's nose and left a wound that later required half a dozen stitches. During the brawl, the coach's suit was ripped in several places.

By then, several Ranger players on the ice raced over to assist their coach. One or two vaulted over the protective glass (not an easy feat) and jumped into the fray with flying fists. Sparks flew from skate blades and fans scattered in all directions as the number of pugilists doubled and the brawl spread.

Policemen moved in to quell the disturbance and peace was eventually restored.

If Francis thought he was going to escape with no more damage than the loss of a good suit, a bent nose, and a few stitches, he was mistaken. Two days later, he received notice that the fans he'd assaulted were suing him — and the Rangers — for a million dollars.

Five years passed before the case was heard in court. When all the testimony had been heard, the jury filed out. In passing Francis, one of the jurors whispered to him, "Good luck, Emile."

An innocent remark, perhaps, but not a wise one. The judge had overheard and he was aghast. He rapped his gavel and bellowed, "Mistrial!" Two more years passed before a verdict was reached and the jurors sided with the claimants. The second jury awarded them — not a million dollars — but damages of $80,000.

"But that's not the end of the story," Emile chuckles. "While I'm wondering where I'm gonna get 80 grand to pay the three jokers who brought me to court, they all came over and asked me for my autograph."

Gilbert Died, and Came Back to Life

ROUND Manhattan, even now at age 56, Rod Gilbert is still a high-profile hockey celebrity. Kids seek his autograph and oldtimers recall when he was the number one star of the New York Rangers.

Gilbert, when he reflects on his 16 high-scoring years (406 goals in 1,065 games), surely must thank his lucky stars he was able to make a name for himself in hockey. There was a time he would have been happy to get in a season or two. He never once — back then — thought he'd someday be summoned to the Hockey Hall of Fame.

For he's a survivor of two delicate back operations as well as a blood clot that might have cost him his life. During the second back operation, he claims he died on the operating table and endured a mystical out-of-body experience.

In 1960, Gilbert was a teenager in junior hockey, playing for a Guelph, Ontario, club. One night, a brain-dead fan casually tossed an ice cream wrapper onto the ice during a game. Gilbert, skating at full speed, stepped on the wrapper with his skate, crashed into the end boards, and lay writhing on the ice. The result was a back injury that would torment him for the next several years.

During the off season, he underwent major spinal fusion, surgery that kept him off skates for several months. After the operation, he was told that a blood clot had developed in his leg. Gilbert had read about blood clots. Sometimes they were fatal. The surgeons held a conference and debated whether or not to amputate. "I was scared to death," Gilbert recalls. "Not only was my hockey career in doubt, but there was a chance I might leave the hospital with one leg missing — if I left at all." Fortunately the medics were able to dissolve the blood clot and within days, Gilbert was able to start his rehab.

During the spring of 1962, apparently fully recovered, he was back on skates, playing for the Kitchener-Waterloo club of the Eastern Pro League. In April, the Rangers, down two games to nil in a semifinal playoff series with Toronto, counted on Gilbert's fresh legs and booming shot to get them back in the series — a tall order for a nervous rookie playing before the howling mob at Madison Square Garden, the largest crowd he'd ever seen. Game three, won by New York 5–4, was a confidence builder. In game four, Gilbert exploded for a pair of goals and assisted on the winner. His splurge against Johnny Bower of the Leafs, even though the Rangers lost the series four games to two, left New Yorkers rejoicing. They took the good-looking rookie with the dazzling smile and the French Canadian accent to their hearts.

But NHL stardom is never assured, no matter how dazzling the debut. Gilbert recorded 31, 64, and 61 points in his first three seasons on Broadway. Then his wonky back began to trouble him again and the medical verdict was grim; he would have to undergo a second spinal fusion. No way, he said. He challenged the diagnosis and persuaded the doctors to let him play with his back trussed up in a steel brace. After half a season, and with 10 goals to his credit, he limped into manager Emile Francis's office and said, "It's no use. I need the surgery. Let's do it right away so that I'll have time to heal and be ready for next season."

"Good idea," said Francis.

Gilbert went under the knife for the second time on February 1, 1966. And he almost didn't survive.

"I died on the operating table that day," he confided to me recently. "I was gone for maybe three or four minutes and I left my body. It was an amazing experience. I looked down from above the table and I saw them working on me, trying to restore my heartbeat. Emile Francis was there, and when the nurse said,'I think we've lost him,' Emile jumped up and shouted, 'You can't lose him. He's my best right winger. Bring him back!' And somehow they brought me back."

For the next 14 days, Gilbert lay immobilized, suffering intense pain. Finally he was discharged and allowed to fly home to Montreal to recover and prepare his body for another season of hockey.

The Loss of the Red Baron

ON November 26, 1967, Ranger center Gordon (Red) Berenson played a prominent role in the Rangers' 1–0 victory over the visiting St. Louis Blues. Only later did Berenson discover that the Rangers were showcasing him that night, hoping the Blues, or some other NHL team, would take him in a trade.

Despite the fact the ex-college star had scored only two goals in 49 games as a Ranger, Berenson impressed the Blues brass, and the following day an agreement was reached. The Blues would send Ron Atwell and Ron Stewart to New York in return for Berenson and defenseman Barclay Plager. It was one of the worst deals Emile Francis ever made. Berenson would instantly blossom into one of the league's top marksmen. He would score 20 or more goals for eight of the next 11 seasons, enjoy a 17-year career, and earn the colorful nickname "Red Baron" because of his sniping skills (261 career goals). He and Plager became the heart and soul of the Blues and led the team to three consecutive West Division titles.

On November 7, 1968, Berenson set an astonishing personal mark when he beat Philadelphia goaltender Doug Favell six times in a game — to equal a modern-day goal-scoring record. In the 8–0 Blues' victory, the Red Baron became the only player in NHL history to score six goals in a road game.

And it was a former Ranger — Lynn Patrick, then manager of the Blues, who outsmarted Emile Francis in landing Berenson for his expansion team.

Tears Flow as Old Garden Closes

$\mathbb{S}$IXTY-TWO of the greatest players in NHL history were on hand to help close the doors of Madison Square Garden on Sunday, February 11, 1968. In ceremonies that preceded the final game between the Rangers and the Red Wings, the oldtimers skated around the rink while the organist played "Auld Lang Syne." The capacity crowd stood and applauded. Some had tears in their eyes.

Before the opening ceremonies, souvenir hunters began tearing loose signs to rest rooms, exit markers — anything they could get their hands on. At the finish, some tried to rip the seats from their moorings and had to be chased by Garden's police.

Rocket Richard was there, reminiscing in the dressing room about a four-goal night he once enjoyed at the expense of the Rangers.

Former Ranger Wally Stanowski wagered 10 bucks that he'd get a bigger cheer than the Rocket during the player introductions — and he did. When Stanowski was introduced, he raced on the ice and did a couple of lovely figure eights and a pirouette, earning the ovation he needed to surpass the Rocket's.

Goalie Jacques Plante, who played for Montreal and the Rangers, recalled November 1, 1959, and the game in which he introduced the goalie face mask to hockey.

"My nose had been ripped open by one of Andy Bathgate's hard shots. I told Toe Blake, my coach, that I wouldn't go back in the game without the mask I'd been using in practices. Toe didn't like the mask but his only other choice was to use Joe Shaeffer as my replacement. Joe was the standby goalie for the Rangers and Toe had heard that he was a very poor goaltender. So he let me wear the mask. After that, I never took it off [except for one game later that season]. When I came on the ice that night, a Ranger fan yelled, 'Hey, Plante, Hallowe'en is over.'"

Every living member of the NHL's first All-Star team was invited to the closing, as well as players who took part in the first game at the arena on November 25, 1925. Ranger heroes like Lynn and Muzz Patrick, Ching Johnston, Davey Kerr, Bill Cook, and Frank Boucher were there, and when Johnston struggled into his rusty skates, he wrapped them in hockey tape to cover the holes. "These are the skates I took from the team when I left," he said chuckling. In the game itself, the Rangers came from behind to tie the Red Wings 3–3. It seemed fitting that two of the Rangers' finest, Rod Gilbert and Jean Ratelle, as they had so many times in the past, teamed up for the tying goal early in the third period. Ratelle converted Gilbert's pass at the 45-second mark and the red light flashed for the final time in the old building.

Death of Shutout King Tragic and Bizarre

TERRY Sawchuk, one of the greatest goaltenders in NHL history, was 40 years old in that summer of 1970. The Rangers' backup netminder, with an unbeatable NHL record 103 shutouts in his hip pocket, was going through some difficult times. There was a recent divorce from his wife, Pat, mother of his seven children. There was a serious car accident, in which his father, Louis, was injured and lay in a Detroit hospital, encased in casts. The goalie's illustrious playing career appeared to be over — or almost so — for the Rangers made it clear they had no further use for Sawchuk. The man was an emotional and physical wreck.

His was a career that began and ended with tragedy. As a lad in Winnipeg, Sawchuk was there when his 17-year-old older brother, Mike, died of a heart attack. Ten-year-old Terry inherited his brother's old goal pads. Within a year, another brother, Roger, died of pneumonia.

At age 15, Sawchuk packed a couple of shirts into a cardboard suitcase, pocketed a 10-dollar bill his mother gave him, and rode the train to Galt, Ontario, where he took his first strides in junior hockey.

Before long, he moved up to the Windsor Spitfires in a tougher junior league, and at age 18, he was starring with Omaha, a Detroit farm club in the United States Professional League. He was named rookie of the year with Omaha and captured similar honors the following season with Indianapolis of the American Hockey League.

He was called up to the parent Red Wings in 1950 and soon replaced Harry Lumley as the Wings' number one netminder. At the end of the 1950–51 season, he captured the Calder Trophy as top rookie in the NHL. His 11 shutouts and 1.99 goals-against average were an indicator of things to come. In his first five seasons, his average stayed below two goals per game. In 1952, he led the Red Wings through a playoff sweep with eight consecutive wins over the Leafs and the Canadiens. He recorded four shutouts and an incredible goals-against average of 0.62 — allowing just five goals in a masterful postseason performance. In 1955, he was traded to the Boston Bruins but quit the team a year later, claiming his nerves were shot. He returned to Detroit where he played until the end of the 1963–64 season when he was drafted by Toronto. His finest moments as a Leaf were in 1967 when he guided the club to a surprise Stanley Cup victory over Montreal. With NHL expansion in 1967, he was claimed by the Los Angeles Kings where he played for one season before returning to Detroit. The following season, his last, he found himself in a Ranger uniform, backing up Ed Giacomin.

On April 29, 1970, with 20 big-league seasons behind him and staring into an uncertain future, Sawchuk went to a bar in Long Beach — the E and J Pub — where he met Ranger teammate Ron Stewart, then 37. The two players rented a home in the area and often were seen in the popular hangout. The players got into a heated argument over how much responsibility each had to clean up the house they soon would be vacating. After some pushing and shoving, they left the bar and returned to the house at 58 Bay Street.

There, on the front lawn, the argument erupted again and Stewart was shoved and fell on his back. Sawchuk tumbled on top of him. Stewart's knee came up and struck Sawchuk in the midsection. Sawchuk began screaming in pain and the Ranger team doctor, Dr. Nicholson, who lived nearby, was called. He examined Sawchuk and immediately called an ambulance.

In hospital, Sawchuk said, "I tagged Stewart (outside the bar) and knocked him down. He got up and I tagged him again. Then he went home. Ron thought I would cool it but I didn't. When I got back to the house, he was outside and I hit him again and knocked him down. Then I jumped on him but his knee came up and hit me in the belly."

Stewart would say his teammate's death "doesn't make sense. He fell on me, that's for sure. But he took much worse falls on the ice and he always bounced back. Then he trips on me and suddenly his life is ended. There was a barbecue stand on the lawn and he hit himself on one of the protrusions on the cooker — or against my knee. It's like a bad dream when I look back on it." Several days after the incident, Sawchuk's gall bladder was removed. A liver operation followed and on May 20, the goaltender was taken to a New York hospital where another liver operation was performed. But a blood clot developed and moved from a vein into a pulmonary artery. Sawchuk died on May 31.

Ranger general manager Emile Francis said, "The guy was the greatest goalie who ever put on a pad. The heart that couldn't pull him through this time, pulled off miracle after miracle when hockey games had to be won."

Frank Boucher, who began his Ranger career as a player in 1926 and concluded it almost 30 years later as New York's general manager, once said without equivocation, "I've never seen a goaltender to equal Sawchuk."

On June 5, 1970, Ron Stewart and 10 of his Ranger teammates traveled to Berkley, Michigan, to attend funeral services for Sawchuk.

Later that month, a Nassau County grand jury ruled the death of Sawchuk completely accidental. Ron Stewart was cleared of any criminal responsibility in the death of the goaltending legend. District Attorney William Cahn told reporters that testimony from nine witnesses indicated the two players had been involved in a "childish and senseless verbal argument with a lot of pushing and shoving," and that the death was "tragic, senseless, and bizarre."

Ratelle Never Fought, Never Swore

O N May 28, 1981, Jean Ratelle retired from hockey after a 20-year career during which he excelled for two NHL clubs, the New York Rangers and the Boston Bruins. When he left the game at age 40, Ratelle was the league's sixth-leading scorer with 491 goals and 776 assists for 1,267 points. He now holds down 21st position on the all-time scoring list.

Ratelle spent 14 of his 20 seasons with the Rangers, many of them centering the high-scoring "GAG (goal-a-game) Line" with Rod Gilbert and Vic Hadfield.

At his peak, he meant as much to the Rangers as Jean Beliveau meant to Montreal, as Bobby Clarke meant to Philadelphia, or as Gil Perreault meant to Buffalo.

"My friend Jean was every bit as good as anyone I ever saw or played against," said Gilbert. "He was one of those classic players, a real artist on the ice. He could do it all. In fact, he would have been successful at anything he decided to do."

Gilbert knew Ratelle better than anyone in the game. They started playing together as lads in Quebec and were teammates for almost 30 years. In all that time, Gilbert says he never saw Ratelle in a fight — on or off the ice — and he never heard him swear.

The soft-spoken, devoted family man could have taught a course to other players and called it Consistency on Ice. Emile Francis coached him for a dozen years, beginning in junior hockey in Guelph, Ontario. Emile says, "He was really unbelievable. I can't remember him ever having a bad practice, let alone a bad game. He was the most consistent player I've ever seen."

Ratelle was a key player in one of hockey's most shocking and spectacular trades. Early in the 1975–76 season, he was shipped to Boston, along with Brad Park and Joe Zanussi in return for Phil Esposito and Carol Vadnais.

He hated to leave New York. "It was a huge jolt at first," he recalls. I'd lived in New York all those years and I'd never been with any other organization. I always considered the Rangers to be my team."

Incredibly, Ratelle never took a major penalty in two decades of play, and won the Lady Byng Trophy twice for gentlemanly play. His biggest regret? He never played on a Stanley Cup–winning team.

The Sizzling Seventies

THROUGHOUT the seventies, the Rangers were a team bordering on greatness. It was a happy decade for Ranger fans who cheered their favorites on to two Stanley Cup final appearances and five matchups in the Cup semifinals.

The decade began with the Rangers involved in three memorable playoff series against the Chicago Black Hawks in '71, '72, and '73. The '71 series, won by Chicago in seven games, was marked by three overtime goals, two by the Rangers' Pete Stemkowski and one by Bobby Hull. Stemkowski's second overtime winner ended one of the longest games in New York history — a thriller that ended in the third extra frame.

In '72, the Rangers suffered a severe blow when Jean Ratelle, a candidate for the individual scoring title, went down with a broken ankle late in the season. Even so, the Rangers upset Montreal in a series that went six games, then stunned Chicago with a four-game sweep to enter the finals. Unfortunately for New York, the Bruins' Bobby Orr was at the peak of his brilliant career and it was Orr who almost singlehandedly demolished New York's hopes in the finals. The Bruins won in six games, and Orr captured the Conn Smythe Trophy as playoff MVP.

The Rangers upset the Bruins in a '73 playoff series but fell to Chicago in the semifinal "crossover" round.

Phil Esposito, who joined the team in a monster trade on November 7, 1975, made a hard-to-believe comment about a 1979 playoff series. "The high point of the decade was beating the Islanders in the 1979 playoffs," he said. "We eliminated them in the semifinals four games to two and it made up for them knocking the Rangers out in 1975. I played on two Cup winners in Boston but 1979 was just as exciting as anything there. Even more exciting." Really, Phil?

In 1975, the Isles pushed the Rangers aside by winning a best-of-three preliminary series, capturing the third game after 11 seconds of overtime play on a goal by Jean Paul Parise. Parise's marker absolutely stunned the Garden's crowd.

The peak of goalie John Davidson's injury-plagued career was in 1979. In 18 playoff games, he allowed just 42 goals for a goals-against average of 2.28. Davidson sparkled against the Islanders in a semifinal series, won by the underdog Rangers in six games. The Isles had suffered the fewest regular-season losses (15) and accumulated the most points (116). Their ace centerman, Bryan Trottier, was the 1978–79 scoring champ with 134 points and Mike Bossy, his right winger, had scored a league-leading 69 goals. Perhaps those two were looking beyond New York to the Stanley Cup finals. To their consternation, because of Davidson and his mates, the Isles' season was abruptly over.

In the finals against Montreal, a team that finished one point behind the Islanders in regular-season play, Davidson's wonky knee hampered his mobility and his timing. A goalie without full mobility has no chance against shooters like Guy Lafleur and

Steve Shutt. But Davidson's grit and some opportunistic scoring in game one was the talk of the Forum crowd as the Rangers stunned one of the greatest Montreal teams ever assembled by a score of 4–1. One of the stars was Ulf Nillson, who was back in the lineup after breaking an ankle 10 weeks earlier. The Rangers made goalie Ken Dryden look so porous, he was replaced by Bunny Larocque.

Larocque prepared to face the Rangers in game two. But the last shot taken on him in the pregame warmup struck him right between the eyes, knocked him down, and he lay unconscious on the ice. Later, Ranger fans would wonder what might have happened if Larocque had not been rendered hors de combat. Dryden lumbered off the bench and, a little unfocused, quickly gave up a pair of goals. The Rangers became excited. Maybe they could steal a pair at the Forum and sweep the series. That thought had just settled in their minds when the Habs, lashed by coach Scotty Bowman, struck for three goals in eight minutes. Dryden was unbeatable the rest of the way, and Montreal coasted to a 6–2 rout. The momentum was now all Montreal's.

Back in New York, Montreal skated to a 4–1 victory in game three and followed up with a 4–3 overtime win in game four. If there was a turning point in the game and the series, it was Bob Gainey's goal in the third period. He barreled into the New York zone, knocked Dave Maloney flying with a heavy check, and scored the goal that tied the score 3–3. The starch the Rangers had shown in game one was missing in game five at the Forum. New York managed a mere seven shots on goal after the first period, lost 4–1, and watched glumly as thousands of wildly excited Habs fans saluted Montreal's fourth consecutive Stanley Cup triumph.

Dorey First Ranger Deserter

"**Y**OU'LL be a New York Ranger for a long, long time," were the words defenseman Jim Dorey heard when he joined the Rangers in the middle of the 1971–72 NHL season. Traded from Toronto where he had gained a measure of fame for serving a record nine penalties in his initial game on Maple Leaf Gardens' ice, Dorey was concerned about finding a spot on the Ranger roster. He was somewhat reassured when general manager Emile Francis told him Tim Horton had predicted big things for Dorey.

"Still, you've got a very strong defense corps," Dorey told Francis.

"Don't worry, kid. You'll be part of it. And for a long time to come. I'm even going to give you a raise to get you off to a good start with us."

In his first game as a Ranger, Dorey suffered a shoulder separation and was lost for the season.

In July, he shocked the Rangers by jumping to the rival World Hockey Association for an offer he "couldn't refuse."

Dorey told me recently, "By jumping to the WHA, I made a lot of the Rangers wealthy men. After I left, the Ranger brass promptly signed all their star players to huge contracts. And it was all because of me."

Maybe so, Jim. But a fellow named Nick Mileti may have had even more to do with the fat 1972 pay hikes handed the Rangers.

During the summer of '72, Mileti, the owner of the Cleveland Crusaders of the WHA, tried to woo defenseman Brad Park and two other stars away from the New York Rangers. Mileti offered Brad Park, Vic Hadfield, and Rod Gilbert a million apiece to jump leagues. At the time, their average salaries were about $50,000.

The late Bill Jennings, Ranger president, in reminiscing about the war between the leagues, once said he had to make a quick decision. With the loss of three of his top players, his club would surely plummet in the NHL standings. He ran to the bank and renegotiated *all* the Ranger contracts. Park was given $250,000, Hadfield and Gilbert received about $200,000, and all the other players on the roster were given appropriate raises. Overnight, the New York payroll leaped from $750,000 to around $2 million.

"I did things in the WHA I'd never think of doing if I'd stayed with the Rangers," Dorey told me. "After Hartford, I played with Quebec and one night we're up against Birmingham. Their resident tough guy, Gord Gallant, suckered Paul Baxter of our team and Gallant went to the penalty box to serve a major, two minors, and a misconduct.

"The coach made it clear he expected me to do something about Gallant. It was the last time we'd be facing Birmingham because the league was about to fold. But what could I do? The guy would be in the penalty box for all but the last few minutes of the game.

"So I led a four-man rush out of the Quebec zone, then stopped at center ice, right in front of the penalty box. I wheeled and sent a slapshot right at Gallant's head. He ducked and the puck struck a photographer standing behind him, knocking him flat.

"I got out of town right after the game but I'd upset a lot of people and they chased after me, especially the lawyers. Finally, they took me to small claims court and I had to pay a fine of $9,999.99 — the penalty had to be under $10,000 — and that's how I ended my career in the WHA."

From Skate Sharpener to Team President

GLEN Sather toiled for the Rangers from 1970–71 to 1973–74 and compiled a record of 18 goals and 42 points in 188 games. A scrappy, fun-loving forward, there was no indication then that Sather's hockey talents, within 10 years, would carry him to the all-powerful positions of coach, general manager, and president of the Edmonton Oilers.

Some former Rangers recall Sather as an industrious, wisecracking winger. Other teammates remember him as a skillful skate sharpener. During a game one night, coach Emile Francis barked instructions at Sather, who'd been used sparingly.

"I thought Emile wanted me to jump on the ice and stir things up. Instead, he told me to run back to the skate sharpening room and put an edge on one of Jean Ratelle's blades. And I did it, too. I must be the only NHL player who ever doubled as a team skate sharpener."

Hockey's Answer to Namath

ROD Gilbert, in his prime, was often called "the Joe Namath of hockey." The handsome Ranger right winger was forced to stickhandle his way through hordes of female groupies after games. In all of the nightclubs he frequented, a stream of gorgeous women stopped by to say hello or wish him luck. Many made X-rated suggestions that would have brought a blush to the face of Madonna. Others relied on NHL-style elbows, jabs, and hip checks just to get a coveted seat next to him at the bar.

"Namath's women couldn't compete with Rod's," Brad Park once said. "Rod's were always classy, as bright as they were beautiful." A '70s reporter once asked if the word "swinger" described Gilbert, and Park was quick to deny it. "No, no, absolutely not. The guy won't let any woman interfere with his concentration on hockey. I've never seen him treat any woman as anything but a lady — even the ones who can't keep their hands off him. They automatically fall all over him. As for his dates, they're all first class — in looks and everything else. One night after a game," Park recollected, "Rod was showered and shaved and all spruced up. I remember he had on a fantastic-looking suit. And I said to him, 'You got a big date tonight?'

"He said, 'Yeah, a great date. We're going out galvanizing.'

"I said, 'Galvanizing? You sure you don't mean gallivanting?'

"He shrugged and said, 'Don't forget. French was my first language.'"

During that era, a magazine conducted a poll and Gilbert was named as one of the sexiest men in sports. The mail response was incredible. Bundles of love letters filled Rod's apartment, many of them from married women and most of them describing in vivid detail what they'd like to do with Rod "between the sheets."

"Women are the best things in life," Rod told journalist Alan Ebert at the time. "I only wish I knew a way to be with *one* woman — devote the time necessary to be with her — and still play hockey."

He came close to marriage early in his Ranger career — to a gorgeous girl from Thailand. "We split up when I discovered she wanted a regular life and I wasn't ready for that," Rod says.

An actress friend once said, "Rod is the most fantastic lover I've ever been with! He's the only man I know who can make you feel when you're with him that there's no other woman in his life."

Eventually Rod married the Coppertone girl — a dazzling blonde flight attendant named Judy Preston, who was seen on billboards across North America promoting Coppertone products. The marriage failed but a second marriage has been "the best thing that has happened to Rod," says former teammate John Davidson.

At the 1996 Hall of Fame induction ceremonies in Toronto, I told Rod I was writing a book about the Rangers. "Would you mind," I asked him, "if I used a quote about you from one of your former girlfriends?"

"What's the quote?" he answered.

"Well, it's the one your actress friend made — about you being the most fantastic lover she's ever had."

Rod's eyes lit up and he laughed. "Geez, use it," he said. "Be sure and use it. It's a great quote. Hell, that's a lot better than being called a great hockey player."

Rangers Watch as Schultz Pounds Rolfe

(C)AN a one-sided fight determine a series or turn one around? Sometimes it appears that way. Let's go back to the 1974 Stanley Cup playoffs when I was with NBC, working with Tim Ryan and Ted Lindsay on the NBC playoff telecasts, when Fred Shero's Broad Street Bullies climbed to the top of the heap and the Flyers' Dave "The Hammer" Schultz bloodied many a nose with his flying fists.

In the 1974 semifinals, the Flyers met the Rangers in a memorable series, one involving skill, speed, and finesse (Rangers) versus brawn, bullying, and intimidation (Flyers). In that era, Fred Shero's Flyers were a menacing band of hard-nosed pros who showed a remarkable determination to win at all costs and with one goal in mind — to become the first expansion team to win the Stanley Cup.

"The Hammer," bold, strong, and fearless, riding a high, was convinced that one tough fighter, a brawler who could thoroughly intimidate, could decide a game or a series with a few solid punches. He relished the thought of his next assignment — pummeling the New York Rangers in the semifinals.

He bided his time in what proved to be a thrilling series. The Rangers showed much more grit than had the Flyers' earlier opponents, the Atlanta Flames. When Schultz and the other Flyers whacked the Blueshirts with their sticks and gloves, they got whacked in return.

Schultz would later admit he had a target in mind — Brad Park. "I always thought Park had too high an opinion of himself," he wrote in his book *The Hammer*. "He was a snob on the ice. In the sixth game I caught up with him. I checked him and knocked him down. Then I stood over his body. I was worked up. I wanted more of Park. I worked myself free of a linesman, and while the other linesman held Park down, I belted him four good ones in the stomach before the officials pushed me to a neutral corner. The fight had a bit of a personal grudge in it, and lots of blind rage."

The series went to a seventh game. By then, Schultz had settled on another player, the Rangers' sturdy defenseman Ron Harris. He confessed he actually gnashed his teeth on game day, anticipating a rousing battle with the unsuspecting Harris.

But hockey is full of surprises. Midway through a scoreless first period, Schultz darted to the Ranger net where he was confronted by big Dale Rolfe and Brad Park. Fleetingly, he thought of clobbering Park again but suddenly Dale Rolfe was in his face, towering over him.

At six foot four and well over 200 pounds, Rolfe had the size to be an enforcer — a tough guy. But he was bereft of a mean streak and everybody knew it. It wasn't in his nature to be a brawler — there was no fury, no menace, in his makeup. That's why it came as a total surprise when he started swinging at Schultz. Typically, Schultz exploded in rage. His short, devastating punches — almost all of them landing — splat! splat! splat! — knocked the stuffing out of Rolfe. Eight, 10, a dozen punches, thrown with stunning force, left Rolfe reeling in shock and in pain. He fell to the ice gasping, blood streaming down his face.

None of the Rangers appeared anxious to come to Rolfe's aid. The Flyers stood around, not smirking perhaps but confident that their teammate's rampage, his furious attack, would enhance their chances of victory. No Ranger could witness Rolfe's humiliation and not be adversely affected by it.

Rolfe would say bitterly, "I remember that nobody from the Rangers stepped in to help me. Nobody. I'll never forget that."

One Ranger on the ice who wanted to step in was Ed Giacomin, the goaltender. But he'd received strict orders from coach Emile Francis to stay out of fights. "Above all," said Francis, "don't be the 'third man in' and take a foolish penalty."

Giacomin said, "Poor Dale was pulverized. The beating he suffered took the stuffing right out of us."

The Flyers prevailed 4–3 to win the game and the series. They moved on to the Stanley Cup finals against Boston — a series they would capture in six games, triggering the wildest celebration in hockey history.

The Rangers could only wonder what might have been and how victory had been snatched away by the Flyers and their bloodthirsty goon.

"It isn't worth it if you have to maim someone to win a game or the Stanley Cup," said Brad Park, the Hammer's nemesis. "It's a game, it's a sport, it's entertainment. It's not World War Three."

Seiling Lashes Fans

ONE night in 1974, over 17,000 fans witnessed Ranger defenseman Rod Seiling performing dreadfully against the weak California Golden Seals. And they started to boo. When he coughed up the puck for a goal, they booed. When he lunged at a Seal — and missed, they booed louder.

After the game, Seiling, a veteran of 11 NHL seasons in New

York and an assistant team captain, bitterly denounced the boo-birds. "Bleep them," he said. "Bleep every one of them."

With those words, Seiling closed the door on his career as a Ranger. Manager Emile Francis tried to trade him. No takers. He placed him on waivers. The last-place Kansas City Scouts had first crack at him and said no thanks. The Washington Capitals (who would win eight games that season) snapped him up for the $30,000 waiver price.

"I can't believe that's all we got for him," Bill Fairbairn, his former teammate, would say. "Not even a player in return."

For Seiling, the agony caused by the fans who vilified him, and whom he in turn despised, was finally over. He would play five more seasons in the NHL, with four different clubs, before retiring in 1979.

In Dryden's View

MONTREAL goaltender-turned-author Ken Dryden (he handled both chores superbly) took a sabbatical from the NHL in 1973–74. Dryden was unhappy earning $80,000 per season with the Habs while less talented puckstoppers around the league were netting $200,000 or more, so he threw off his pads and walked away. During his year away from the game, Dryden had time to observe the performances of several NHL clubs and offered the following comments about the Rangers.

"The Rangers are a strange team. I mean they seem to play along at an even level. They're always quite good, seldom great. They don't rise to any peaks and they don't have slumps. They're in a groove. When they run into a club that's a bit down, they win. When they run into one that's high, they lose.

"Unlike the championship teams I've seen, they don't have individuals who'll peak during a playoff series — play at a higher level than usual, get inspired or whatever. Walt Tkaczuk does a bit, I guess, but he's sort of a negative guy, most effective nullifying somebody."

Ranger fans who recall that era would probably agree with the man who played on six Stanley Cup champions in eight years and now serves as president of the Toronto Maple Leafs.

Little Agent Leaves His Mark — Big Time!

HE was just a little guy, about five foot three, but he was glib — very persuasive. In the mid-seventies, this former sportswriter with *Newsday* convinced about 40 hockey players he was the best man around to look after their off-ice careers. He was Richard Sorkin, player agent.

Sorkin was one of the first agents to scour the junior leagues in western Canada, pen in hand, signing top prospects like Lanny McDonald and Tom Lysiak. He negotiated large contracts for his clients and he arranged for their salaries to be sent to Richard Sorkin, Inc. He promised a total package of financial services. He made deposits, paid their bills, and doled out allowances that took care of their everyday needs.

Ron Greschner was a top Ranger prospect who showed utmost faith in Sorkin. But Greschner's money, like the cash "Slick" Sorkin collected from his other clients, wasn't safely invested in blue-chip stocks and mutual funds as Greschner and the others thought it was. Sorkin was gambling with their money and blew half a million dollars in the shaky stock market of the time. When his concern over losses turned to panic, he blew another half million wagering on sports events — trying to win it all back.

Ron Greschner went to buy a new car one day — a Corvette. When he tried to pay for it, he discovered he was broke. Lysiak, McDonald, Bob Nystrom of the Islanders, and others made the same discovery. They called for an investigation and agent Sorkin, the little man with the winning smile, was charged with fraud and brought to trial. He was found guilty and sentenced to three years in jail.

Sorkin served 11 months of his sentence and became a painting contractor on his release. It took three years for Greschner to make up for the losses he'd suffered. While others cursed the little swindler, Greschner showed compassion. "I almost feel sorry for the guy," he said. "I'm not pissed off at him. And he served his time — almost a year."

A Stunning Loss in Overtime

BY the spring of 1975, the New York Islanders had made some spectacular advances up the NHL ladder. They had leaped from 30 points in 1972–73 (their first NHL season) to 56 points in 1973–74 to 88 points in 1974–75. The new kids on the block, coached by Al Arbour, were on the rise. Their 88 points were good enough for a second-place tie with the Rangers in the rough-and-tumble Patrick Division. The Islanders, bolstered by the addition of 1973 first-round draft choice Denis Potvin, and a 1975 trades with Minnesota that brought them J.P. Parise on January 5 and Jude Drouin on January 7, were pitted against the Rangers for the first time in a playoff series — a two-out-of-three affair.

No longer were the Islanders pushovers for the Rangers or for any other club. By the spring of '75, the two New York teams, playing in the same division, had developed an intense dislike for each other.

The Rangers were favored in the series. Coach Emile Francis had playoff veterans Rod Gilbert, Jean Ratelle, and Eddie Giacomin on his roster. He could rely on Brad Park defensively and he liked the toughness of Pete Stemkowski, Ted Irvine, and Jerry Butler. But Francis had his detractors. He was accused of piloting a team of "fat cats," players who had signed lucrative contracts — some, the highest in history — to avoid a mass exodus to the WHA. The underdog Islanders figured the Rangers had a soft underbelly and were ripe to be taken. This was a team that had soared to 109 points in 1971–72 and produced three of the top 10 NHL scorers in Jean Ratelle (46 goals), Vic Hadfield (50 goals), and Rod Gilbert (43 goals).

A year later, the Rangers had slipped to 102 points with only Ratelle (number six) listed among the league's top 10 pointmen. The following season (1973–74), the Rangers fell below 100 points (collecting 94), and only Park (number nine) could be found rubbing elbows with the top 10 marksmen.

In 1974–75, the Rangers won more games than the Islanders (37-33) and outscored them (319 to 264). The Rangers' goal total was a new club record, as was their total of 84 power-play goals. But the Isles were stingier, giving up only 221 goals (55 fewer than the Rangers), the third-best goals-against mark in the NHL.

Ranger fans scoffed at Potvin's barbs and bristled at his cockiness. They reminded the young defenseman that in 17 meetings between the teams, or since the Isles ventured into the NHL, the Rangers had registered 13 wins, three losses, and a tie. And in the season just ended, the potent line of Ratelle, Gilbert, and Vickers (replacing Hadfield) had amassed 113 goals. The Isles' top scoring hope was Potvin himself, who led his team in scoring with 76 points.

The Rangers held home-ice advantage in the short series and opened with a flourish, whipping two quick goals past Islander goalie Chico Resch. Then the Rangers took some foolish penalties, allowing the Isles to get back into the game. Billy Harris opened the third period with a power-play score, Jean Potvin caught Eddie Giacomin wandering far out of his net, beat him to the puck, and eased it into the open cage to knot the score, and rookie Clark Gillies barreled past two defenders to wrist a shot past Giacomin for the winning goal at 13:30.

"We didn't die and they did," chuckled Denis Potvin afterwards. He smiled again the following day when Jack Chevalier, covering for the *Philadelphia Bulletin*, wrote: "The Islanders proved that wet-behind-the-ears is better than egg-on-the-face."

"We'll stuff it down the Islanders' throats in game two," vowed Ranger defenseman Ron Greschner. And two nights later in Uniondale, the Blueshirts did, walloping the Isles 8–3 in a game that saw the two clubs set a record for most penalties in a playoff game — 50.

In game three at Madison Square Garden, the Rangers stumbled badly out of the gate. Big Clark Gillies scored a first-period goal and Denis Potvin, number one on the Ranger fans' hate list by now, collected a pair of goals in the second period. A full house at the Garden sat in stunned disbelief when the third period opened with their heroes trailing by three. But hardrock winger Bill Fairbairn brought them to their feet with a lovely goal at 4:44 and then another at 13:27. A mere 14 seconds later, Steve Vickers scored and the crowd erupted in glee. But the Isles settled down and the score at the end of regulation time was 3–3.

The overtime period ended in shocking fashion and in record-breaking time. The Isles propelled the puck into the Ranger zone. Steve Vickers attempted to clear but Jude Drouin got his stick on the rolling disc. Jean Paul Parise scooted in front of Giacomin and Brad Park allowed him plenty of ice there. It was as if Parise stood on a welcome mat.

Drouin took a quick shot on net, Parise deftly directed it past Giacomin, the red light flashed, and at the 11-second mark the Rangers were finished, their Cup hopes shattered. The Isles celebrated their first ever playoff series win and established a record for post-game brevity.

Hours after the debacle, the Rangers were still reeling. Derek Sanderson said bitterly, "The Islanders aren't as good as the Atlanta Flames. Trust me, they won't win another game." Steve Vickers added, "That was the most embarrassing defeat I've ever suffered."

The outcome convinced general manager and coach Emile Francis he'd better think seriously about the wisdom of retaining both jobs. Rumors surfaced that Francis would hire Harry Howell to fill the coaching position. Howell, the only Ranger ever honored with a "night" at Madison Square Garden (until then), was extremely popular. But he had his critics, too. Some suggested he might be too soft on the high-priced Ranger stars. Ron Stewart's name emerged after the 42-year-old veteran of 21 NHL seasons with six different clubs made a name for himself coaching Springfield in the AHL. Because Stewart guided the Indians to a Calder Cup triumph after a fourth-place finish, Francis offered him a two-year contract to move up to the NHL. The new Ranger mentor quipped, "We'll have to beat up on the Islanders in the preseason and establish our claim again."

Stewart soon became aware that beating up on the Islanders might take some doing. After eliminating the Rangers, Al Arbour's upstarts had dumped Pittsburgh with an amazing comeback, losing the first three games and winning the next four. They almost duplicated their stunning feat in the follow-up series versus Philadelphia, losing the first three, then winning three in a row, only to lose the deciding game 1–0. The Flyers went on to capture the Stanley Cup in 1975, their second in a row.

Ranger Rejection Leaves Giacomin Stunned

IT was a bombshell. That's the word Eddie Giacomin used to describe it. It was his sudden rejection by the Rangers after 10 seasons of loyal service. He was a beloved Ranger, the team's heart and soul, an extraordinary goaltender who had been a five-time All-Star and Vezina Trophy winner. His daring, roving style, darting swiftly from his net to snare loose pucks and lash them up the ice to teammates, combined with his acrobatic saves, made him the darling of the Garden crowd from 1966 through the mid-seventies.

"I was amazed, disappointed, shocked, all of those things," he said of the cruel trick played on him that Hallowe'en night in 1975.

Emile Francis, under pressure from team owners to make some changes, placed Giacomin on waivers, and the Detroit Red Wings snapped him up. Giacomin was flabbergasted at the news. He recalls shaking Francis by the hand but was unable to speak a single word. It was as though Francis had grabbed him by the throat, not the hand.

Two days later, the Red Wings skated out on New York ice to face the Rangers. Coach Doug Barkley had planned to use Jim Rutherford in goal but wisely switched to Giacomin at the last minute, knowing the Ranger players would have trouble firing their best shots at their long-time friend.

When Giacomin skated out for the warm-up, the fans went wild. The gray-haired goalie could barely see for the tears that filled his eyes. His gaunt body trembled with emotion. Chants of "Ed-dee, Ed-dee" drowned out the anthem and rained down on him after every save, easy or hard.

The Red Wings leaped into a 4–0 lead as the Rangers floundered. A kid named Wayne Dillon scored the first goal on Giacomin and the crowd groaned. Many booed. Dillon was so upset he skated over and apologized to his former teammate.

Brad Park said, "If you ever saw a team intentionally lay down for a game, that was it. We felt so strongly about Eddie. That was a game that we did not want to play. We did not want to shoot on him. And it's true guys like Dillon and Steve Vickers apologized to Eddie when they put the puck past him."

The Red Wings won the game behind Giacomin 6–4. He left the ice completely drained. A standing ovation followed him to the visitors' dressing room. When he stepped on the scales inside, he found he'd lost 13 pounds during the contest.

Reporters, some as visibly upset as the fans, wrote about his amazing career as a Ranger and the bizarre path he took to the

NHL. Ironically, he might have been a Red Wing from the beginning if he hadn't been such an unlikely prospect.

As a teenager, Giacomin was cut by a Red Wing–sponsored team in Hamilton. He returned to his hometown of Sudbury, Ontario, and played with the Bell Telephone club in the city league. Two weeks before the season ended, his brother Rollie, five years older and also a goalie, received a call from Washington of the old Eastern League. Could he come down and fill in for a netminder who'd been injured?

"Not me. Not interested," said Rollie. "Why not give my kid brother Ed a shot? You won't regret it."

"Well, okay," was the answer. "Send him down. We'll take anybody. We've only five games left to play and we're out of the playoffs."

Giacomin headed for Washington, won all five games, and the next season was invited to try out with Providence. During the off-season, however, he suffered severe burns in a house fire and was advised by doctors to forget about hockey — permanently. The advice fell on deaf ears. Giacomin had once promised a schoolteacher that he'd play goal in the NHL one day and he intended to keep that promise.

He played in the minors with the Clinton Comets and the New York Rovers before clicking with Providence in the AHL, where he starred for five seasons.

Meanwhile, in New York, Emile Francis faced a dilemma. He could no longer rely on temperamental Jacques Plante as his goalie and Marcel Paille wasn't the answer, either. He decided to gamble on Giacomin and delivered a bag of bodies to Providence — three players and Paille — to land him.

Eddie's promise had finally been kept, his boyhood dream realized. He had made it — all the way from the midnight league in Sudbury to the NHL.

His rookie season as a Ranger was horrendous, and Francis began to wonder if he'd made a huge mistake. Giacomin won eight games, lost 19, and his goals-against average was a disappointing 3.66. Francis dispatched him to Baltimore where he began to show his old-time form.

In 1966–67, he was back and won the starting job in training camp. But Cesare Maniago, a proven veteran, battled him for the position and it was only when Maniago was injured one night and refused to go back in the game, that Giacomin became the number one goaltender. He won 30 games that season — tops in the league.

During his decade in New York, Giacomin won more games (226) and rang up more shutouts (49) than any other netminder in Ranger history.

Despite his successful start as a Red Wing, he was unhappy in Detroit, a team going through a state of upheaval. In January of 1978, Wings' GM Ted Lindsay told him he'd been placed on waivers — and there were no takers.

A year earlier, he had been promised the Ranger coaching job by president Bill Jennings, but Jennings was overruled by Sonny Werblin, who selected Fred Shero instead.

Phil Esposito didn't forget his old friend. One of Phil's first moves as general manager of the Rangers, in July of 1986, was to sign Giacomin as his goaltender coach.

After an 11-year exile, Eddie was back where he belonged, where he would hear the roar of the crowd once again. First, there was a rousing welcome-home salute on opening night, 1986, when he was asked to drop the first puck of the new season. Then there was an even greater ovation on Eddie Giacomin Night when his jersey was retired (joining Rod Gilbert's high above the crowd) and once more in 1987, in Toronto, when he was inducted into the Hockey Hall of Fame.

Three years later, when Neil Smith replaced Esposito as general manager and allowed new coach Roger Neilson to select the assistant coaches, Neilson asked Wayne Cashman to remain but Ed Giacomin's contract was not renewed.

Potvin Critiques the Rangers

BY the beginning of the 1974–75 NHL season, the rivalry between the New York Rangers and the New York Islanders was intense. Ranger fans resented all the attention the upstart Islanders were receiving, especially their young hotshot defenseman and number one draft choice, Denis Potvin. Never shy with his opinions, Potvin became "Denis the Menace" to Ranger supporters. Unlike most rookies in the NHL, who traditionally are seen but not heard, Potvin pulled no punches and was more candid than Allan Funt. He had a lot to say about the Rangers, about Brad Park, and even about Bobby Orr of Boston, then universally recognized as hockey's premier defenseman.

Potvin jabbed at Orr by saying, "I refuse to agree that Orr at his best contributes more to his club than I do — or that he was the best ever."

When the subject turned to Park, Potvin said, "By the time the season had ended, there wasn't much doubt that I had caught up to Park. I was named to the first All-Star team and he wasn't. When they compared me with Orr I felt it was an honor, but Park? By then I was contributing more than Park."

Potvin showed his disdain for the Rangers by saying, "For some reason they were a club that we knew could be pushed around and even intimidated if we manhandled them in the right way." In his book, *Power on Ice*, Potvin wrote: "There seemed to me to be a definite pattern for the care and mishandling of a Ranger player. They were called "fat cats" for a very good reason: Madison Square Garden was paying them more money, as a team, than any other NHL club, yet they gave little in return. The obvious conclusion to me was that the Rangers played for the money and nothing else. The typical Ranger seemed to be a skater who lacked drive, who missed the extra

Bill Gadsby (here aiding Gump Worsley) played 20 seasons in the NHL but was never on a Stanley Cup winner. — Hockey Hall of Fame

Left to right: Lynn and Muzz Patrick with Gordie Howe, a 1967 winner of the Lester Patrick Trophy.
— Public Archives of Canada C 29550

During the 1960s, goaltender Gilles Villemure won 96 of 184 games for New York.

When the NHL doubled in size in 1967, a new Madison Square Garden became home to the Rangers early the following year. — New York Rangers

A bruised Jean Ratelle: he was the first Ranger to score over 100 points in a season.

Despite two delicate back operations, Rod Gilbert enjoyed a Hall-of-Fame career, scoring a team record 406 goals.
— Robert B. Shaver

Eddie Giacomin won more games (266) and racked up more shutouts (49) than any other netminder in Ranger history.
— Hockey Hall of Fame

Emile Francis was a popular manager and coach of the Rangers. He joined the club in 1964 and was replaced by John Ferguson in 1976.

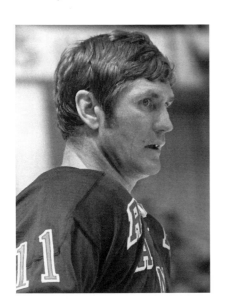

Vic Hadfield became the Rangers' first 50-goal scorer in 1971–72.
— Robert B. Shaver

Steve Vickers was a Calder Trophy winner in 1972–73.   — Robert B. Shaver

Defenseman Dale Rolfe was pummeled by Flyer tough guy Dave Schultz in the 1974 playoffs. It was a turning point in the series, won by Philadelphia. — Robert B. Shaver

Defenseman Brad Park was a key player in the deal that brought Phil Esposito to New York in 1975.

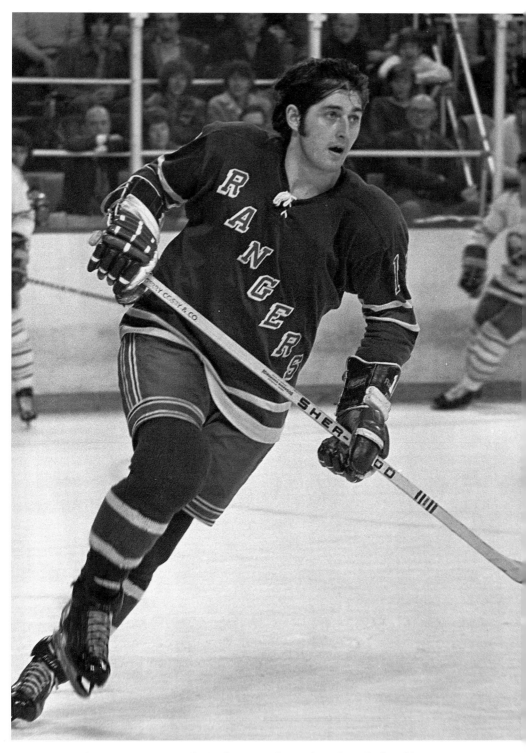

Born in West Germany and raised in Canada, Walter Tkaczuk played in 945 games as a Ranger, from 1968 to 1981. — Robert B. Shaver

Anders Hedberg joined the Rangers in 1978 and collected 78 points in his first season on Broadway.
— Robert B. Shaver

With his long hair and good looks, Ron Duguay was a Ranger heartthrob. He scored 40 goals, a personal best, in 1981–82.

Nick Fotiu, a native New Yorker, became one of the most popular of all the Rangers.

Phil Esposito ended his brilliant playing career as a Ranger, later serving as the club's general manager from 1986 to 1989. — Robert B. Shaver

A two-time winner of the Norris Trophy, defenseman Brian Leetch won the Conn Smythe Trophy in 1994 when he led the Rangers to the Stanley Cup.

— Bruce Bennett Studios

Neil Smith (left) hired Mike Keenan as Ranger coach in 1993. Together they guided New York to the 1994 Stanley Cup, before Keenan left, signing with St. Louis.

— Bruce Bennett Studios

Wayne Gretzky and Mark Messier, great friends and great players, were reunited on July 20, 1996, when Gretzky signed a two-year contract with the Rangers.

— Bruce Bennett Studios

step necessary for victory. Everybody on that club seemed to diddle-daddle a lot and become depressed easily if the puck didn't bounce their way.

"The Rangers had always seemed to be this way, as far back as I can remember. The Rangers never showed me that extra tenaciousness that the Canadiens or the Bruins have always had."

Potvin saved a parting shot for Emile Francis. "One factor that was a constant with the Rangers for as long as I could remember: Emile Francis. More often than not, he had held the jobs of both general manager and coach of the Rangers — which I think is the problem. A manager must keep his distance from the players. He's the guy who negotiates contracts, makes trades, and handles other affairs that frequently inspire the anger of the players. The coach, by contrast, should be a close, father-like figure. The two functions rarely meld well together. Francis coached and managed the Rangers from 1965 through 1975 and never won a championship."

Esposito Learned to Love New York

I T all began in the fall of 1975 when Boston superstar Bobby Orr hurt his knee. Bruin manager Harry Sinden began looking around for another top defenseman to replace Orr. When he asked around and discovered Ranger manager Emile Francis would give up Brad Park — for an aging but still productive Phil Esposito, it wasn't long before a major trade was completed. Francis shipped popular Jean Ratelle, Park, and minor leaguer Joe Zanussi to the Bruins in return for Esposito and defenseman Carol Vadnais.

Esposito and Vadnais were jolted by the deal. Espo — because he thought Sinden had promised him he wouldn't be traded and because he hated New York, and Vadnais because he had a no-trade clause in his Bruin contract. A furious Esposito told Sinden, "Harry, you make me puke." In Vadnais's case, the Rangers hurriedly found some cash to persuade him to waive the no-trade clause.

Esposito left Boston with regrets. He told a reporter, "I regret not signing with Vancouver of the WHA. I would have had the same kind of deal Bobby Hull got in Winnipeg. A million bucks in the bank and a five-year contract at $300,000 per. Then another five years at $250,000. And I turned it down for Boston. A month later, Harry Sinden says I'm gone, traded."

Esposito admits it took some time — over a year — to adjust to life with the Rangers. "But when I did," he says, "I really got to love the place and the good things it had to offer."

Esposito showed only flashes of his old-time form with the Rangers. His best moments came in the 1978–79 season when he led his new team to the Stanley Cup finals against the Montreal Canadiens. The Rangers lost in five games.

At age 38, he felt he was slipping a notch and the big thrills were behind him — the huge victory for Team Canada over the Soviets in 1972 with Espo supplying the leadership, the two Cup wins in Boston in 1970 and '72, and the Rangers' dash to the finals in '79.

Then, midway through the 1980–81 season, Espo was gone. He played his final game at the Garden against the Buffalo Sabres and when he was introduced to a sellout crowd of 17,500, the crowd cheered his name for over four minutes. He fought back tears as he told the crowd, "I've had a wonderful career and I'm sorry it has to end. When I was a kid growing up with my brother Tony in Sault Ste. Marie, I never dreamed I would make it to the NHL. I never thought I would do things I've done. Now that I've done them, I'm proud of them."

Teammate Walt Tkaczuk took the microphone and drew a laugh when he said, "Phil, I want to thank you for the nine miserable years you gave us while you were in Boston and the five wonderful years you've given us as a Ranger in New York."

Gordie Howe stepped to center ice and said, "Phil, you are such a class guy. We're really going to miss you."

In a press release, the NHL noted that Esposito was the first player to crack the 100-point barrier (in 1968–69). He totaled at least 55 goals in five consecutive seasons and he enjoyed his greatest season in 1970–71 when he scored 76 goals and 152 points — records later erased by Wayne Gretzky. He retired with 717 career goals and 873 assists.

Following his retirement, Espo remained in New York and became an analyst on Ranger telecasts. When asked about his hockey beginnings, he would say, "My most embarrassing moment? That's easy. When I was a kid back home, I had to go to the bathroom something awful during a game. But it was my turn to go on the ice. Wouldn't you know, I wet my pants. Did my mother give me heck when I got home."

When John Ferguson was general manager of the Rangers, he had mixed emotions about Esposito. Ferguson could never forget how Espo had led Team Canada to a stunning victory over the Soviets in 1972. On the other hand, he blamed Espo for persuading him to trade with Boston for Ken Hodge, an Espo crony and linemate. Ferguson gave up Rick Middleton for Hodge in what he calls "the worst deal in hockey history." And he blamed Espo and Rod Gilbert for the friction that was so often evident in the Ranger dressing room. Ferguson called them "clubhouse lawyers" and maintained they were always fighting among themselves, with half the team siding with Gilbert and the other half supporting Espo.

THE FERGUSON, SHERO, PATRICK, AND ESPOSITO ERA

First to Get Five

ROOKIE forward Don Murdoch was two weeks shy of his 20th birthday and two weeks into his first season with the Rangers when lightning struck in Minnesota. On October 12, 1976, Murdoch matched an NHL record set three decades earlier by Toronto's Howie Meeker when he clicked for five goals in a game against the Minnesota North Stars. All of Murdoch's goals were "pure" markers, whereas two of Meeker's five (he admits it) were tainted — bouncing in off teammate Wally Stanowski. Murdoch's fifth tally came at 19:55 of the third period in a 10–4 New York victory. Unlike Meeker, who won the rookie award as a Leaf in 1947, Murdoch suffered an ankle injury midway through his first season, played in only 59 games, and scored 32 goals. He finished runner-up to Atlanta's Willi Plett in the rookie balloting.

In August 1977, Murdoch ran into major problems when he was stopped by customs officers in Toronto. A routine search led to the discovery of 4.8 grams of cocaine stashed in one of his socks. Five joints of marijuana were found in a cigarette pack in his pocket. The following April, Murdoch pleaded guilty to possession. He drew a sharp reprimand from a Canadian judge and was fined $400. Three months later, NHL president John Ziegler suspended him for a season.

During the trial, Murdoch was afraid he'd go to jail for his crime. He told a friend he'd have skipped the country if he'd been sentenced to a jail term. Then he sounded less than remorseful. "They made it look like I was the only one. There's everybody doin' it (drugs)," he told writer Larry Sloman. "Doctors, lawyers, all kinds of athletes."

When Sloman turned his conversation with Murdoch to girls,

Murdoch said, "Hey, I come from a small town where there might be 10 good-looking chicks in the whole town. And 500 guys going for them. So I come to New York and I used to get sore necks from turning around looking at all these chicks. Anywhere I'd go, all these nice-looking chicks were coming up to me. I didn't have to work up any lines or anything. They'd come up and ask the questions and they'd do all the answering."

One night at Studio 54, Murdoch was dancing with Margaret Trudeau, the estranged wife of the Canadian prime minister. General manager John Ferguson received a call at home from a certain person asking him to point out to Murdoch that his behavior with Ms. Trudeau was inappropriate. Ferguson also discovered that Murdoch's drug use was not confined to New York. He'd been familiar with the product back in Medicine Hat in junior hockey.

Murdoch's sentence was reduced to 40 games — half a season. When he returned, he scored 15 goals in the half season but was never the same player he'd been before, especially during his rookie season. John Ferguson once said of him, "At first, the kid was super. Then, somehow he lost control. He had an overabundance of talent, but he also had an overabundance of immaturity."

J.D. Recalls a Wild Night at the Garden

FORMER Ranger goalie John Davidson is one of my favorite people, a good friend and a great broadcaster. He was a topflight goaltender too, back in the seventies — the only Ranger ever to wear 00 on his jersey. A series of injuries kept him from being a much bigger star than he was.

I asked J.D. if he recalled an incident in his Ranger career that really shook him, one that comes quickly to mind whenever he reflects on games played at the Garden.

"There was a game one night between the Bruins and the Rangers," he says. "Had to be in the late seventies. I remember we were leading by a goal in the third period and we wound up losing 4–3. And we'd lost three or four times before that game, so you can imagine how frustrated and angry I was at the buzzer that night. I believe Madill was the referee and he let everything go. As a result, there were elbows thrown and plenty of slashes and other dirty little tricks, but very few penalties. Our two Swedes, Hedberg and Nilsson, were the main targets for the Bruins. They were punched and pummeled and pushed around. Then, midway through the third period, Ulfie Nilsson got some revenge. On a line change, he slipped up behind Al Secord when Madill was looking elsewhere and knocked Secord's feet out from under him. Secord fell on his ass and the Ranger fans roared their approval. By the time Secord jumped to his feet, Ulfie was sitting on our bench. But Secord had noted Ulfie's number.

"Then, late in the game, Ulfie got a partial breakaway and might have won the game for us. But Gerry Cheevers made a sensational stab at the puck. Seconds later, the game was over.

"I skated toward center ice and Ulfie and the rest of the Rangers were coming toward me. Suddenly Ulfie was sent flying, teeth-first into the ice. Secord had nailed him. I raced toward Secord and drove into him. Within seconds, there were 40 players on the ice all pushing, shoving, punching, cursing. Like a swarm of bees, we moved toward the Boston net, then veered off toward the side boards. The fans who had started to leave raced toward the glass and pounded it with their fists, shouting obscenities at the Bruins.

"Stan Jonathan, a tough little Bruin, got too close, and somehow a fan whacked him in the face. Jonathan's stick flew up and another fan grabbed it. Wouldn't let go. After that, all hell broke loose. I saw Terry O'Reilly vault the boards and cut a path through the fans, who scattered. He went wild. Then Mike Milbury and Peter McNab — big, tough men — followed, thrashing their way into the crowd. One of the Bruins — I think it was

McNab — yanked a guy's shoe off and began beating him over the head with the heel. All kinds of garbage came flying down on those involved. You could hear people screaming. Others shouted, 'Bruins suck! Bruins suck!' Security guards raced in and joined the wrestling match. Suits were ripped and bloodied. I remember wondering how they'd ever put a stop to it, but somehow they did.

"Back in the dressing room, I shook with emotion. My stomach was in knots and my hands were shaking. Dave Maloney, our captain, was in tears. He'd been involved in a bitter argument with Madill, and Madill had called him an asshole. I guess I said a lot of things to the press, talking about the Bruin cheap-shot artists and how Ulfie had been suckered.

"The crowd was still wild with rage and gathered outside the Garden, daring the Bruins to come outside and fight. I don't know how long the Bruins had to wait in their dressing room until it was safe to emerge.

"It's funny. There's another thing I remember about that night. Ron Duguay was concerned because he'd arranged for Cheryl Tiegs to attend the game. I think it was her first time. Ronnie had told her, 'Come to a Ranger game. You'll love it.'"

A Sparkling Debut at the Forum

O N February 25, 1978, Ranger goalie Hardy Astrom was a surprise starter against the powerful Montreal Canadiens at the Forum. The Swedish import was making his NHL debut against the NHL's strongest club. The Habs were riding a 28-game unbeaten streak and the Rangers, in the past six seasons, had come away from the Forum with only a single point in regular season play.

If Astrom was nervous about facing the shots of Guy Lafleur, Steve Shutt, Yvan Cournoyer, and the rest of the Flying Frenchmen, he didn't show it. He turned in a splendid performance. His mates, meanwhile, scored twice each period and New York skated off with a 6–3 victory.

Unfortunately for Astrom, his NHL career spiraled downhill after his initial stellar performance. After a season with New York, he returned to Sweden for a year and then played a couple of seasons under coach Don Cherry in Colorado. Over the years, Cherry has ridiculed Astrom, calling him "my Swedish sieve" and claiming that "in practices I'd shoot dinky little shots from center ice and beat the guy."

Astrom finished his undistinguished career with 17 victories in 83 starts and a goals-against average of 3.74.

We Loved You, Nick

A fourteen-year-old boy, a New Yorker named Nick Fotiu walked into Gerry Cosby's sporting goods store one day and bought a cheap pair of skates.

"These'll get me started in hockey," he told the clerk. "And when I get real good, I'd like to play for the Rangers."

It wasn't long before Fotiu, playing for the New Hyde Park Arrows, was the star of his league. But getting to the games wasn't much fun. It meant a two-hour ride on the subway, a sometimes frightening journey. Nick carried a hatchet in his hockey bag, to scare off any punks who might accost him, demanding his wallet, or worse, his skates.

In time, his play caught the eye of New York Ranger general manager Emile Francis, who arranged for him to play with the Cape Cod Cubs of the North American Hockey League.

By the early '70s, the New England Whalers of the fledgling

World Hockey Association, hungry for U.S. talent, signed Fotiu from under the nose of Francis. Two years later, Fotiu was acquired by the Rangers, attaining the goal he'd set on the day he bought his first pair of skates at Cosby's. When he made his NHL debut at Madison Square Garden, he became the first native New Yorker to wear a Ranger jersey.

"This is where I was meant to be," he told reporters. "This is going to sound crazy, but I was sitting at a Ranger game one night and God talked to me. He said, 'Nicky, someday you'll be down on that ice.' I never doubted Him and look — now it's come true."

Fotiu never pretended to be a stylish performer like Rod Gilbert or Jean Ratelle. His approach was all slam, bang, and bash, bopping around the rink with boundless energy. He loved the crunch of body contact and he proved to be a fearless fighter. He was never a scorer, never masqueraded as one. He popped in nine goals in three seasons, a meager total that would have earned less popular players a constant chorus of boos and catcalls.

There were no jeers for Nicholas Evlampios Fotiu. Ranger fans adored him.

He was always the last man off the ice after warm-ups. He would gather pucks and throw them to youngsters eager for a souvenir. Some pucks he hurled 150 feet into the upper reaches of the building, for he remembered when he, giddy with excitement, had occupied one of those seats. He recalled how he'd stand in line for hours outside the building for the privilege of buying a ticket to a Ranger game.

In the spring of 1979, he had a chance to play on a Stanley Cup winner. His Rangers faced the Montreal Canadiens in the finals. Fotiu was crushed when the Habs won the series four games to one.

He was even more despondent a few days later when the Rangers failed to protect him and he was reclaimed by the Whalers in the Expansion Draft.

"Leaving New York was very hard," he says. "It was a terrible blow. Still, I got to play with legends like Gordie Howe and Dave Keon. Imagine me, Nick Fotiu, a kid from New York, a roller hockey player, skating with two of the greatest players in the game."

Ranger fans missed big Nick. They missed his charisma, the pucks he'd throw to the crowd, the jolt he'd give his teammates when he leaped into the action, stirring them to greater effort with his rambunctious style.

Larry Sloman, in his book *Thin Ice*, said of Fotiu: "Look, he didn't start skating until he was 15, okay, so how could he skate like all those frogs, fancy and stuff, huh? So Nicky did the next best thing, he just built up steam like a runaway freight train, and if you happened to be in his path, look out. How did he stop? That's what boards are for, ain't they?"

In January 1981, a trade brought him back again, back to New York and the arena where he felt he'd always belonged. On March 11, 1986, he was traded to Calgary where he played for parts of two seasons. He went to the Flyers for 23 games in 1987–88 and was given a one-time trial with Edmonton in 1988–89. But he failed to score a goal and his 12-year NHL career was over.

Bizarre Behavior of Freddie the Fog

FEW of us in the media could ever figure Freddie the Fog. That's coach Fred Shero, of course, who guided the Rangers from 1978 to 1980. He was as elusive as Howard Hughes, as mysterious as Mandrake.

Here are some examples of Sheroisms:

1. In 1979, the Rangers played the Islanders. During the game, Shero tapped one of his players on the shoulder, pointed out on the ice, and said, "Who's that player — number 18?"

"That's Westfall," was the answer. "Eddie Westfall."
"Not him," said Shero. "Number 18 on our team."

2. When the Rangers acquired Cam Connor in a trade, Shero told reporters, "We can always use another defenseman."
   When a puzzled scribe pointed out that Connor was a forward, a left winger, Shero shrugged and said, "Well, we can always make a defenseman out of him."

3. In 1978, Shero arrived at the Garden for a game. There was just one problem. The game was between the Knicks and the Celtics. The following day, pretending he'd planned to see an NBA match, he told his players he really enjoyed the action.

Son of Namath

"THEY often compared me with Joe Namath," Ron Duguay says, speaking of the Jets' quarterback whose off-field amours matched his gridiron glamor.

Like Namath, Duguay, who grew up in Sudbury, and who played six years with the Rangers beginning in 1977–78, had some impressive names in his little black book — celebrities like Cheryl Tiegs, Patti Lupone, Farrah Fawcett, Bianca Jagger, and Cher. The handsome kid from the Nickel Belt had come a long way from the Sudbury bar scene where a celebrity was Stompin' Tom Connors singing "The Good Old Hockey Game."

In a 1981 issue of *Forum* magazine, Duguay candidly discussed his sex life in Manhattan. Game days, he made it clear to the interviewer, were for celibacy. "Sex before a game weakens me," he declared. "Some guys it doesn't affect. Me — when I go in the corners my legs get rubbery."

While *Forum* readers devoured the intimate details of Duguay's nightlife, another publication, one of those supermarket news-papers, focused on his relationship with Cher, calling them "a sizzling disco duo."

The paper revealed that Cher, 35, and Duguay, 24, met at the trendy disco Studio 54, where they often danced until the wee hours. An insider spotted the couple on the dance floor and con-fided: "Cher and Ron were very passionate on the dance floor and off. She kissed him, snuggled close to him. Ron held her close and often leaned down to kiss her and whisper in her ear."

A third interview in artist Andy Warhol's *Interview* magazine mentioned Duguay's white Cadillac, his gold speedboat, and the TV ads he was appearing in for Sassoon jeans. "Doogie" — that's what cafe society was calling the curly-topped player — "never wears a helmet."

"I can't see myself wearing a helmet," he confided, "because I just love going out there with that freedom, your hair flowing in the air, the whole bit. The helmet really bothers me . . . it's tight and you start sweating and it's itchy."

Warhol was most concerned about his nose. "Your nose is so beautiful, Ronny. You can't wreck it."

Writer Scott Cohen expressed concern about another body part. "How about guys skating without a cup?"

"A guy would be crazy to go out there without a cup," said Doogie, surprised at the question. "That'd be risking everything."

Team leader Phil Esposito warned Duguay to be careful. "What you can't forget," said Phil, "is that if you don't perform on the ice, you can kiss everything else goodbye. Never forget that you're a hockey player first. There are a million guys out there who can model."

Doogie's first big season was in 1981–82. He scored a career high 40 goals in 72 games and added 36 assists for 76 points. The following season, in 72 games, he produced only 19 goals. A per-sonality clash developed between the 26-year-old right winger and new coach Herb Brooks. Perhaps the final straw was Duguay's penchant for arriving late for practices. Each time he was tardy, Brooks would fine him $50. Late in the season, when his teammates kidded him about the costly fines, he asked them how many workouts there were left. When told there were four, he calmly wrote out a check for $200. That kind of attitude did not sit well with Brooks. In the off-season, to Duguay's shock, he was traded to Detroit.

Detroit owner Mike Ilitch quipped, "If I didn't get the best goal scorer in the league, I sure got the prettiest."

Duguay turned in two outstanding seasons with the Red Wings. He tallied 80 points in 80 games in his first year and 89 points the following season. From Detroit he went to Pittsburgh, then back to the Rangers for a partial season, and finally to Los Angeles where he retired in 1989.

Herb Brooks Could Never Top the Olympic Miracle

AS a player, Herb Brooks was a member of the U.S. Olympic team in 1964 and 1968. Four years earlier, he was deprived of winning a personal gold medal when he was the last player cut from the victorious squad at Squaw Valley. At the University of Minnesota he earned a degree in psychology and, beginning in 1972, he coached his alma mater in hockey for seven seasons. His team captured national championships three times — in 1974, 1976, and 1979.

His golden moment came in 1980 when he coached the U.S. Olympians to a stunning upset of the Soviets — the Miracle on Ice — at Lake Placid, an event televised by ABC and viewed by millions. In a movie made for television about the triumph, veteran actor Karl Malden was cast (miscast is more apt) as Brooks, who called the production "bloody awful. I couldn't sit through it. Malden must have done it just for the money."

Brooks spent a few months coaching in Switzerland before joining the Rangers as head coach in 1981. He was lured to

Broadway by general manager Craig Patrick's offer of a $250,000 contract — the highest coaching stipend in NHL history. Ironically, Patrick had served as Brook's assistant during the unforgettable race to Olympic gold in 1980.

Brooks got off to a fabulous start behind the Ranger bench, guiding the club to a second-place finish in the Patrick Division in 1981–82, an impressive 18-point improvement over the previous season. He was named Coach of the Year by the *Hockey News*, and by 1984, his team finished 42-29-9, the team's best showing in 11 seasons.

By then, the love affair with Brooks was over and after a 15-22-8 start in 1984–85, Patrick fired him. "I wasn't surprised when he was let go," said Ron Duguay, who was then a Detroit Red Wing. "You can only fool people so long. Things haven't changed since I was there and that means the relationship between the coach and players is about the same."

Goaltender Eddie Mio, who was also traded to Detroit, added, "I can't say I'm sorry. The chemistry didn't seem to be working."

Brooks blamed Patrick and Ranger president Jack Krumpe. He said he had asked for more input on the people who went up and down in the organization and he didn't get it. "It came to a head and the rest is history."

Hockey writers Stan Fischler, Rich Friedman, and others concluded that Brooks talked his way off the Rangers. They said he bitched about his players, about Craig Patrick, about everything, but always off the record.

One of his comments about defenseman Barry Beck appeared in the *New York Times* under Craig Wolff's byline: "Brooks calls Beck a coward."

Brooks denied he said it. A few days later, he told me emphatically during an interview on *Hockey Night in Canada* that he had not said it. On the same day, Beck told me he didn't believe that Brooks, or any coach, would describe him as cowardly. It didn't make sense. Nevertheless, several reporters said they were convinced the quote was accurate. One said, "If I could print all the stuff Brooks has told me he'd have been gone before this."

Mark Pavelich: Who Needs Him?

IN 1980, Mark Pavelich, a five-foot-eight, 170-pound center-man from Eveleth, Minnesota, went from the ecstasy of an Olympic gold-medal victory — the U.S. team's "Miracle on Ice" at Lake Placid — to the gloom of hockey unemployment. Who wanted him? Almost nobody.

While several of his Olympic teammates moved to high-paying jobs with NHL clubs, Pavelich waited in vain for the phone to ring. He knew, of course, why no teams called. He'd been branded too small for the roughhouse play of the NHL.

In order to continue in hockey, Pavelich had to leave the country he'd served so well. He packed his hockey gear and his fishing poles (he's an all-star fisherman) and flew to Switzerland where he joined the Lugano team in a mediocre league. Herb Brooks, who'd become an international celebrity after coaching the Americans to their stunning triumph at Lake Placid, was coaching a team in Davos, a few miles away over the winding mountain roads.

Pavelich was a star in the Swiss league, collecting 73 points in the 60 games he played. Still, he longed to display his goal-scoring skills where it really mattered — on home soil and in front of NHL fans.

His chance came the following season. Herb Brooks returned to North America to coach the Rangers. Brooks recommended Pavelich, and the diminutive free agent scrawled his signature on a contract.

The playmaking skills Pavelich displayed in his rookie season made his former critics ("I tell you, the kid's too small.") squirm with embarrassment. Pavelich chalked up Ranger rookie records in each scoring category — most goals (33), most assists (43), and most points (76). One night he even scored five goals in a game, to equal a club record established by Don Murdoch. He suffered a broken ankle in the second game of the 1984–85 season, and he was shocked when his mentor Herb Brooks was fired early in 1985. Under new coach Ted Sator his ice time was cut back, he lost his confidence, and he began to wonder about his future in the game.

On March 10, 1986, he failed to show up for a Ranger practice. That week, he told reporter Frank Brown of the *Daily News*, "They (the coaching staff) don't know what they're doing. They really don't. Well, that's their problem. And that's the reason I'm going to retire." And he walked away.

What wasn't revealed at the time is that flashy teammate Reijo Ruotsalainen almost walked with him. Weeks later, Ruotsalainen would say, "I almost went with Pav. Maybe I was a little stronger. He couldn't cope with the pain that he had in his head."

In July, Ruotsalainen announced he would leave the Rangers to play for a Swiss team. Pavelich said he intended to play for Dundee in Scotland. And a third Ranger, Barry Beck, citing "philosophical differences" with the coach, said he would not be back if Sator were to remain behind the bench.

New Ranger general manager Phil Esposito successfully blocked Mark Pavelich from playing in Scotland and traded Ruotsalainen's rights to Edmonton. And Beck wound up with Los Angeles for a final season. Later, Esposito invited Pavelich to come to New York and "talk things over" but Pavelich declined, saying, "I think the game has passed me by."

Too bad. His Ranger career was far too brief.

Ranger Larouche Misses Third 50-Goal Season

PIERRE "Peter Puck" Larouche was an 18-year-old phenom when he broke in with the Pittsburgh Penguins in 1974–75. He scored on his first shift in the NHL and collected 31 goals as a rookie. He was surprised when he was named runner-up to Atlanta's Eric Vail (39 goals) as NHL Rookie of the Year.

Everything surprised him then: his first goal, his popularity, even the fact he was drafted. The following season he scored 53 goals and collected 111 points. Lucky Pierre was the youngest sniper ever to surpass 50 goals in a season.

An outspoken young man, he developed a habit of criticizing management in Pittsburgh which did not endear him to his employers. As a result, during the 1977–78 season he was traded to Montreal where he recorded a second 50-goal season and played on two Stanley Cup–winning teams. Larouche was traded to Hartford in 1982 and when he became a free agent the following year, he was happy to sign with the Rangers. No player had ever scored 50 goals in a season with three different teams but Larouche came close. With 48 goals and three games left to play, he broke his wrist and his chance to create history was over. It was his final high-scoring season.

Larouche drove his coaches wild with his deplorable defensive play, but his ability to keep the red light glowing made him their golden boy. He played another four seasons for New York and when his scoring touch vanished, so did he.

His career stats are impressive: 395 goals and 427 assists for 822 points in 812 games. A point-a-game average is something most NHLers strive for but few attain. Larouche made it look easy.

The Esposito-Bergeron Feud

P HIL Esposito said he fired Michel Bergeron late in the 1989 season because the coach went over his head, complaining to Garden's sports boss Jack Diller that Esposito's many trades had not helped the team. Michel Bergeron's blunt response was, "That's bull. Espo is talking nonsense. I was fired for only one reason — because Esposito wanted to coach the Rangers himself.

"Let's tell the truth," added Bergeron. "That's the only reason he dumped me." He hinted that Espo timed the firing so that he could take over and win some playoff glory. If so, the move backfired when the Rangers lost four straight to Pittsburgh.

Bergeron's days may have been numbered after a 4–3 loss to Detroit in March. Bergeron stated his players were "scared" of their opponents that night.

"The guy defied me at every turn," Espo told Frank Brown of the *Hockey News*. "Why, he even tried to begin trade talks by calling another team's coach. That's not insubordination? Then he goes over my head to Diller. More insubordination. Well, bleep him. I took enough."

Esposito said he was encouraged to hire Bergeron in the first place by the people around him. There's never been a deal like it — giving up $100,000 and a first-round draft choice for another team's coach. "I didn't want to give up so much but my scouts and other people around me said, 'Phil, you should do it.' So I did. Then he comes here and I didn't like the way he treated people — the players, the press, and even myself."

Bergeron's reputation for being tough on first-year players caused at least one Ranger prospect, college star Eric Bennett, to decline a Ranger contract. Two players in Denver, the Rangers' affiliate in the International League, turned down an opportunity to join the team in New York. "No thanks," they said. "Bergeron has ridiculed us in the past. We don't need any further humiliation."

Walt Poddubny, a Ranger under Bergeron in 1987–88, predicted his career as a Nordique was over — with Bergeron back in control. "How am I supposed to play for him after the things I heard he said about me? Obviously I can't coexist with Mr. Bergeron."

Esposito had the final word as he contemplated a return to the broadcast booth. "As for me firing Bergeron because I wanted to coach again — that's ridiculous," Esposito said. "I never wanted to go behind the bench again and that's the truth of it."

Lafleur Comes Back

"I think the odds of Guy Lafleur making a comeback in the NHL are not very good," Ranger general manager Phil Esposito said on a hot August day in 1988. "But the guy asked me for a chance. He's a Hall-of-Famer and a true superstar of hockey. He's only 37. What have I got to lose?"

Lafleur said, "People think I'm crazy but I have to try this. I don't want to wake up one morning when I'm 50 and say to myself, 'Why didn't I give it another shot?' Remember, big Gordie came back and he was a lot older than I am." Guy was referring to Gordie Howe, the only other player to return to pro hockey after his Hall of Fame induction. Howe returned at age 45 after a two-year absence to play alongside his two sons Mark and Marty for Houston in the WHA, concluding his NHL career with Hartford as a 52-year-old grandfather.

So three days after Lafleur was inducted into the Hockey Hall of Fame in Toronto, he reported to the Ranger training camp.

In camp, youngsters 15 years his junior treated him with utmost respect and admiration. Some couldn't resist asking him for autographs. Most were awed by his presence and his accomplishments. He had played 14 seasons for the Montreal Canadiens and had scored 518 goals. He was a two-time winner of the Hart Trophy as MVP, a three-time winner of the Art Ross Trophy as scoring champion, and he'd played on five Stanley Cup–winning teams. In 1977–78, he scored a career high 60 goals.

Three or four other NHL clubs had shown a passing interest in Lafleur. Rogie Vachon, general manager of the Los Angeles Kings, almost signed him. He considered him as a possible linemate for Wayne Gretzky, only to conclude that Lafleur, who'd been out of the NHL for almost four seasons, was too old and too rusty to make it back.

Nobody faulted Vachon. Four years away from the game is an eternity.

It was on November 24, 1984, when Lafleur, a 14-year veteran, decided to walk away from the Montreal Canadiens. He had scored a mere two goals in 19 games to begin the season, and his ice time had been reduced by coach Jacques Lemaire to about nine minutes a game. After he retired, the Habs offered Guy a job in the organization at $75,000 per annum, but he soon quit that position as well, complaining that he'd been treated like "an office clerk."

He talked openly of being manipulated into retirement by the Canadiens. "They played games with me, got me to retire, and gave me a nonexistent job to keep me quiet. It cost me four years of my life."

Away from the game, he was depressed and irritable. He went for long walks and drove his red Jaguar recklessly and at dangerous speeds. "When a man drives as fast as Guy does, that man has a death wish," his father Rejean declared. "But then, the purpose had gone from his life."

The purpose returned, when, risking injury and embarrassment, he came back to the NHL with the Rangers. Perhaps money was a motivator as well. Lafleur knew that if he managed to play in 100 more NHL games, he'd qualify for a lump sum payment of $250,000 at the age of 55.

"I'm rooting for him," said Ranger forward Pierre Larouche, owner of jersey number 10, a numeral made famous by Lafleur. "I'll gladly give up my number to him if he wants it."

At training camp, Ranger coach Michel Bergeron was impressed with Lafleur's skating, his skills, and his upbeat attitude. Bergeron and general manager Phil Esposito didn't hesitate in giving him a passing grade — and a two-year contract.

The highlight of Guy's comeback season took place at the Montreal Forum on the night of February 4, 1989. A broken bone in his foot had kept him out of the Ranger lineup for an October visit to the Forum when fans paid scalpers as much as $500 just to see him come out and wave to the crowd.

On February 4, he did more than wave. He rocketed a puck into the net behind Patrick Roy midway through the second period and the Forum rocked to its foundations. Shouts of "Guy! Guy! Guy!" saluted the goal. Never had a goal scored by a visiting player been so acclaimed. A few minutes later, he stripped the puck from Petr Svoboda, whipped another goal past Roy and once again was showered with cheers and applause. The goals were his 11th and 12th of the season (he would finish the year with a respectable 18) and his first goals on Forum ice since October 25, 1984. Even though the Rangers lost the game, Lafleur collected three points and was the hero of the night. Scalpers, it was said, demanded up to $1,000 for a pair of tickets to witness the Flower's return to the scene of his past triumphs.

Lafleur's career as a Ranger ended on a bizarre note. When Phil Esposito fired coach Michel Bergeron on April Fools' Day, 1989, before the Rangers' 79th game, the Rangers were in shock, especially Lafleur who had been well treated by Bergeron. The dismissal came as a complete surprise. Two years earlier, Esposito had delivered $100,000 and a first-round draft choice to the Quebec Nordiques to land Bergeron and had signed him to a three-year contract. But the Rangers went into a late-season swoon and finished the 1988–89 campaign with five straight losses. For the final two defeats, Esposito stood behind the bench, taunted with barbs like, "Espo, you suck," and "You and your fat ego, Phil."

Esposito's gamble failed miserably in the first round of the 1989 playoffs. His players, dismayed by Bergeron's sudden ouster, lost four straight games to the Pittsburgh Penguins, a team making its first playoff appearance since 1982. Lafleur scored one playoff goal against the Penguins. It was his last marker as a Ranger.

The team's owners, meanwhile, were growing disenchanted with Esposito. He had paid dearly for Bergeron, then feuded with him openly. He had made 44 trades in his three years at the helm, compiling a so-so record of 107-107-26 and his team had lost two playoff series. On May 24, he was told to clean off his desk and get out. With that decision, Lafleur decided not to return for another season in New York.

In September, he resurfaced in Quebec City, a city he loved. There as a teenager in junior hockey, he had scored 130 goals one season and led the Quebec Remparts to the Memorial Cup. There he was reunited with Bergeron, who'd been installed as coach, a mere 13 days after being dismissed by Esposito.

"I am happy to be back in Quebec," he said. "I left New York because the two men who brought me there, Bergeron and Esposito, are no longer with the organization." Quebec compensated the Rangers for Lafleur's signature with cash and a fourth-round draft pick.

But his star was fading fast. Chain-smoking, drinking, playing around with women, and fast cars, an on-the-edge lifestyle common among true superstars, had taken their toll. After two seasons with the Nordiques (62 points in 98 games), at the end of the 1990–91 season, Lafleur retired to one of the loudest and longest standing ovations in the history of his native province.

"I can leave in peace now," he said. "I no longer need fast cars and women. I don't need the cheers and the crowd chanting my name. And I thank the Rangers for their role in this. They gave me a chance to come back and fulfill a final dream. But this is the end of hockey for Guy Lafleur."

THE NEIL SMITH ERA

Hats Off to Smith . . . and His Mother

I T'LL soon be a decade on the job for Ranger president and general manager Neil Smith, a man who excels in snapping up intelligent draft picks, free agent signings, and bartering for free talent. During Smith's term with the Rangers, his club has won three division titles, two President's Trophies, and one Stanley Cup. After Smith's 1993–94 Rangers swept to a stunning Stanley Cup victory in 1994, his name was elevated to the lofty status enjoyed by Ranger legends of the past, men like Lester Patrick and Frank Boucher.

The oddity is, Smith's mother might have been able to do the job just as well. His mother, Margaret Topp Smith, now Margaret Cater of Don Mills, Ontario, was a star player with one of Canada's women's teams in the thirties. She was Neil's first coach (his father died at age 50), teaching him to skate, stickhandle, and shoot. Her lessons paid off when he became an All-American defenseman at Western Michigan University. In 1991, he was inducted into the school's Hall of Fame, the first hockey player so honored. His mother still gives him advice on how to run the Rangers, some of which he takes seriously because "my mother sure knows her hockey."

Why shouldn't he listen to his mother? This is a woman who grew up in Winnipeg, studying the Hextalls and the Colvilles and playing on outdoor rinks with several future NHL stars.

From her Don Mills home, she isn't shy in offering comments and opinions on current Rangers.

"There are three or four I really like," she says, "not because they are star players, which they are, but because they are great people. Like Adam Graves and Mike Richter and Brian Leetch. Brian Leetch is an amazing person on and off the ice. I watched him develop into a complete defenseman, one of the very best. And of course Mark Messier and Wayne Gretzky are terrific too. I never liked Mark very much when he played with Edmonton, a rough, tough cookie if I ever saw one. But I love him in a Ranger uniform."

What about coach Colin Campbell?

"Another good person. I really enjoy and respect Colin and his wife, Heather. I remember when Neil was first hired by the Rangers. I got the nicest letter from the Campbells, saying how proud I must feel and that I must have done all the right things for Neil when he was growing up. It was a lovely letter and much appreciated. You don't forget little things like that."

Neil's mother still watches endless hours of hockey on television, thanks to the satellite dish he gave her, and on videos Neil sends her from New York. And she lets her son know when she sees mistakes on the ice.

"I wish I could see more hockey," she says. "During the Memorial Cup I wanted to follow Christian Dube of Hull, a Ranger draft choice, and Eric Savard of Oshawa."

What does she think of controversial Mike Keenan, former Ranger coach?

"You know, you meet Mike one-on-one, and he's the nicest person in the world. You say to yourself, 'How could anyone not get along with this man? He's great.' Then you hear other people talk about him and you have to wonder if they're talking about the same person. Neil prides himself in being able to get along with everybody. But not with Mike. Mike, he said, was impossible."

After college, Neil turned professional and played briefly with Indianapolis of the WHA, the Saginaw Gears and the Dayton Gems of the IHL, and the Hampton Gulls of the ECHL. When he realized his skills were unlikely to win him a big league berth, Smith moved to New York and became a salesman for a giftware firm.

Enter Jimmy Devellano, then with the Islanders, the man who'd scouted Smith in junior and college hockey. Devellano invited Smith to an Islanders-Rangers game one night and asked him to do some pre-scouting for the Isles. No pay, just expenses. "I'm your guy," said Smith, delighted to play even the smallest role for an NHL team.

Smith's scouting reports were so thorough, so impressive, that when Devellano moved to Detroit as general manager, he invited Smith to come along, this time as a bona fide scout. The pay was not impressive — $22,000 a year — but it sounded good to Smith. He jumped at the opportunity.

The following season he was named director of Detroit's farm system. A year later, he was director of scouting and general manager of the Red Wings' farm club in Glens Falls, New York. His team won the Calder Cup during his first year on the job.

In 1989, the Rangers were seeking a new man at the helm as Phil Esposito had just been released. Smith was interviewed for the position and the Ranger moguls were impressed with the plan he'd prepared. He suggested some bold moves: how to rebuild the farm system, who else to hire, and who to let go. He was handed the reins on July 17, 1989.

In his first three seasons in New York, Smith guided his team to a pair of first-place finishes and the runner-up spot once — the three best consecutive finishes in Ranger history. The NHL governors and general managers named him Executive of the Year in 1992, and the Rangers promoted him to the position of team president and general manager. A year earlier, he had acquired from Edmonton Mark Messier, one of the world's greatest players, and free agent Adam Graves from the same club. These key additions led to the most remarkable campaign of them all — the 1993–94 season with a club record of 52 wins and 112 points and the fourth Stanley Cup in franchise history.

On July 21, 1996, Smith boldly signed Wayne Gretzky as a free agent, reuniting the tandem of Gretzky and Messier. Ranger fans are hoping these two future Hall-of-Famers will finish their splendid careers in Ranger livery.

Neil Smith has enjoyed phenomenal success as the guiding force behind the Rangers. And all because he listened to his mother.

Summer of Rage,
Winter of Wins

IN his first three seasons as president and general manager of the Rangers, Neil Smith saw his club finish atop the Patrick Division twice. Add a second-place finish in 1990–91, and you have the best three consecutive finishes in club history.

But the playoffs failed to bring that long-awaited Stanley Cup, and Smith, after his club was shamed by Washington in the first round of the '91 postseason, made a number of changes. He shipped out veterans Kelly Kisio, Brian Mullen, and Bernie Nicholls, and brought in one of hockey's greatest stars, Mark Messier.

Smith's summer of rage led to a winter of wins with Messier providing leadership in abundance. Messier finished fifth in league scoring with 107 points and guided his mates to first place overall with 50 wins and 105 points, seven more than Detroit. The last time the Rangers won the overall title was in 1942.

Messier captured the Hart Trophy for the second time, edging Patrick Roy of Montreal in the voting. Brian Leetch (102 points, ninth in scoring) captured the Norris Trophy over Boston's Ray Bourque — a huge accomplishment. Tony Amonte scored 35 goals, one shy of Tony Granato's record for a Ranger rookie. Adam Graves was signed as a free agent and scored a career high 26 goals. Sergei Nemchinov, the Rangers' first Russian player, scored 30 goals in his first season, Mike Gartner had 40, and James Patrick amassed a career high 71 points.

It was a glorious regular season marred by a walkout of players at the end of the campaign and another crushing disappointment in the playoffs.

The Rangers squeezed by New Jersey in the first round and were leading powerful Pittsburgh 2–1 in games in round two. In the second match, Adam Graves broke Mario Lemieux's hand with a slash, putting Lemieux out of the series. Graves was suspended for four games and was called a "goon," a "thug," and an "assassin" by outraged Penguin fans. Lemieux threw some petrol on the flames by suggesting that Graves's hit was deliberate and that the Rangers had a "contract" out on him. With Lemieux gone, Ron Francis picked up the slack and was the key to yet another Ranger playoff defeat, Pittsburgh winning four games to two.

Stan Fischler, writing in the *Hockey News*, fingered goalie Mike Richter for a blown goal in game four of the series. "Richter is lucky hockey isn't baseball," wrote Fischler. "When it comes to publicizing historic moments, his boo-boo on a Ron Francis 65-footer in game four of the Patrick Division final would go down in sporting infamy. In terms of impact, it can be compared to Mickey Owens's classic dropped third strike in 1941. That mishap triggered a ninth inning two-out rally that torpedoed the Brooklyn Dodgers' World Series hopes."

In the gloom of defeat, no one dared predict or even suggest that Stanley Cup glory was a mere two years away.

Richter, All-Star MVP

I N 1990–91, Mike Richter and John Vanbiesbrouck shared the goaltending chores for the New York Rangers and set a record by alternating at the position for 76 games. Ultimately, with expansion, general manager Neil Smith had to choose between the goaltenders and he opted for Richter, the native of Abington, Pennsylvania, and former college star at Wisconsin. Richter promptly turned in a phenomenal season in 1993–94 with a league high 42 wins (a franchise record) in 68 games, five shutouts, and a 2.57 goals-against average. He finished the regular season on a high and racked up consecutive shutouts over the

Islanders in the first round of the playoffs. He played a total of 23 playoff games and was a key performer throughout as the Rangers marched to the '94 Stanley Cup.

In January 1994, at the annual All-Star game played in New York, he put on a dazzling show. He replaced Patrick Roy in the second period for the Eastern Conference and handled 21 shots, five of them off the stick of Vancouver's Pavel Bure. His efforts earned him MVP honors and a new truck.

In September 1996, Richter excelled on the world stage, providing Team USA with superb netminding as the youthful Americans toppled Team Canada 5–2 in the third and deciding game for the World Cup championship at Montreal. As tournament MVP, Richter walked away with a new Harley Davidson motorcycle and the respect of hockey people everywhere. Calgary's Theo Fleury said, "The guy should never have to buy another drink for the rest of his life."

Because the World Cup games were not telecast in American markets, few hockey fans in the United States were able to witness or appreciate Richter's smashing performances. Baseball pennant races and football training camps took precedence over the hockey showcase. What a shame. American fans, swelling in numbers every season, missed the most meaningful victory by an American team in the history of the game. And Richter was the key to it.

Graves Guns for Fifty

WHO'D have thought that Adam Graves would blast 50 goals into NHL nets during one season of play? Certainly not his previous coaches in Detroit and Edmonton. In those hockey hotbeds, he'd produced seasons of seven, nine, and seven goals.

Ranger general manager Neil Smith certainly didn't envision

50-goal potential in Graves whenever he saw him play. But he saw a lot to like in the hustling left winger and didn't hesitate to woo him from Edmonton when Graves became a free agent in the summer of '91. Once he donned Ranger colors, Graves's career took off like a rocket.

He scored 26 goals in 1991–92 and 36 goals the following season. Midway through the 1993–94 campaign, when Ranger fans began clamoring for the Stanley Cup, Graves began his assault on a record dating back 22 seasons — Vic Hadfield's team mark of 50 goals.

Ironically, it was back in Edmonton, before Oiler supporters who recalled Graves's futile efforts to collect as many as 10 goals in a season, where he first tied and then shattered the long-standing Hadfield mark.

It was late in the season, on March 23, when Graves converted a two-on-one first-period pass from Mark Messier, flipping the puck over the sprawl of former teammate Bill Ranford. It was goal number 50!

Graves's teammates would have leaped on the ice to pound his back and shower him with congratulations, but NHL rules forbid such impulsive behavior. That would have to wait until he scored number 51, the league moguls ruled.

Graves didn't keep them waiting. Less than three minutes later, he banged a second puck past Ranford and there was a mass exodus from the Ranger bench. Adam Graves had wiped Hadfield's name from the Ranger record book. By season's end, he had established a new mark of 52.

The modest Graves said he was happy to get away from the media attention his scoring feat attracted and added, "I should cut the record-breaking puck into 25 pieces and give them to my teammates."

Neil Smith admitted he hadn't consulted a psychic or played any hunches when he signed Graves. He had no inkling the winger's goal production was about to soar. "I figured he might be good for 30 to 35 goals, but over 50? That is a pleasant surprise."

Lindros Almost a Ranger

ON June 30, 1992, NHL arbitrator Larry Bertuzzi made the biggest decision of his life. Bertuzzi ruled against the New York Rangers in deciding the future home of teenage wonder Eric Lindros. That home would be Philadelphia.

Perhaps you've forgotten the bizarre series of events that put the Rangers in the running for Lindros's name on a contract.

It began when Lindros thumbed his nose at the Quebec Nordiques, who drafted him number one overall in 1991. Lindros made it clear that he would not sign with the Nordiques no matter how they pleaded and begged, or how much money they threw on the table. Incidentally, the money was considerable for a failing franchise — $55 million over 10 years. It didn't impress Lindros. He sat out a year, playing amateur hockey.

Twelve months later, Quebec general manager Marcel Aubut threw up his hands, and agreed to dispose of Lindros to the highest bidder. It was the most expensive auction in the history of hockey. It was also the most bizarre.

Aubut decided the most attractive offer for Lindros came from the Flyers. It included veteran goaltender Ron Hextall, 28, center Peter Forsberg, 19 (drafted sixth overall by Philadelphia in '91), defensemen Steve Duchesne and Kerry Huffman, center Mike Ricci, left wing prospect Chris Simon, Philadelphia's first choice in 1993 (Jocelyn Thibault), another future draft pick, and $15 million.

Aubut told Rick Curran, Lindros's agent, that the deal had been consummated and that Lindros was now a Flyer.

But ten minutes later he backpedaled and said that he'd negotiated a better deal with the New York Rangers, one that included goalie John Vanbiesbrouck, forwards Tony Amonte (35 goals), Doug Weight (8 goals), Alexei Kovalev (a prospect), three first-round draft picks, and $12 million. The Philadelphia deal, Aubut declared, was off.

But hold the phone. The Flyers lodged a protest and the mess landed in the lap of arbitrator Bertuzzi. Bertuzzi's decision to award Lindros to the Flyers came 10 days after Aubut's double-dealing. It required five days of testimony to sort things out. Bertuzzi ruled that Aubut had made an enforceable deal with the Flyers before he was tempted by the Rangers' offer.

In hindsight, one wonders if the Rangers are thankful the Lindros decision went against them. If they'd have been awarded Lindros, would they have paid millions more for Mark Messier or Wayne Gretzky? Would they have won the Stanley Cup in '94 with Lindros leading a decimated lineup? But one could also argue that Lindros will still be a superstar long after Messier and Gretzky are gone from the scene.

Mike Keenan's Greatest Gift Was to New York

ICHAEL Edward Keenan was born in Toronto, October 21, 1949. As a lad, he and his family moved to Whitby, Ontario, where his dad, Ted, worked for General Motors. Michael showed some leadership ability early in life: in church, in the classroom, and on the hockey team.

He played hockey well enough to earn a scholarship to St. Lawrence University at Canton, New York. There, as team captain, he was described as "a hardworking forward without a whole lot of talent." On campus, he gained renown as one of the originators of a rock band "Nik and the Nice Guys" which still performs, playing Superbowl gigs, etc. — but without Keenan, the original lead singer in the band. Keenan went on to earn his master's degree in education at the University of Toronto. He played inconspicuously on the university's Canadian championship team in 1973.

After playing a couple of seasons in minor pro hockey (Roanoke Valley), Keenan took a schoolteacher's job in Oshawa, Ontario, and began coaching a junior B team in that city. Coaching appealed to him and his teams had winning records. Still, there was little to indicate his style was unique, that his talents would propel him all the way to the NHL, that his name would one day grace the Stanley Cup.

In 1979, he took over as coach of the Junior A Peterborough Petes where a handful of more famous coaches, namely Scotty Bowman, Gary Green, and Roger Neilson, had preceded him. Under Keenan's firm hand, the Petes went to the Memorial Cup finals in 1980.

Scotty Bowman, then coach and general manager of the Buffalo Sabres, hired Keenan to coach the Sabres' AHL franchise in Rochester. He led the Rochester Americans to the Calder Cup in 1983, his third season there. When Bowman failed to elevate him to the Sabres, he returned to college hockey at the University of Toronto and coached his team to the Canadian Intercollegiate title. His collegians won 41 games, lost only five, and were 9–0 in playoff competition.

The Philadelphia Flyers had been following his string of successes and came calling in May 1984. Keenan arrived in the NHL less than two weeks after Bobby Clarke retired from a 15-year playing career. Clarke was Keenan's first general manager.

In his initial NHL season, Keenan's Flyers finished atop the NHL standings with 113 points. But his team lost out in the Stanley Cup finals to Edmonton. Mike Keenan was named Coach of the Year.

The Flyers finished second overall for the next two seasons. In year three with the Flyers, Keenan won his 150th NHL game, reaching that plateau faster than any coach in history. Twice his teams made it to the Stanley Cup finals.

By then, "Iron Mike" had become a nickname, and he'd earned a reputation, not only as a winner, but as a critical coach who terrorized some players. One young Swede, Thomas Erickson, complained that he was verbally abused by Keenan to the point where he quit the NHL and returned to Sweden.

In his fourth season in Philadelphia, he faced a rebellion.

Players stopped performing for him. After the Flyers blew a 3–1 playoff lead over Washington and were ousted, the players asked management to fire Keenan — they said they'd had enough of him.

Clarke fired him. Chicago snapped him up but only after Keenan made owner Bill Wirtz promise to name him general manager by 1990–91.

Keenan led the Hawks to the Stanley Cup semifinals in 1989 and 1990, but he was constantly feuding with superstar Denis Savard.

In 1990, as Chicago's new general manager, he engineered a trade with Montreal, snaring Chris Chelios, a troubled defenseman, who was on the verge of greatness, in return for Iron Mike's aging nemesis — Savard.

In time, Keenan disagreed with former general manager Bob Pulford on several issues and finally delivered an ultimatum to owner Wirtz — "It's Pulford or me." Wirtz opted for Pulford, and Keenan was fired.

On April 17, 1993, Keenan was named head coach of the New York Rangers and promptly took the Rangers — last-place finishers in their Division in 1992–93 (79 points) to first place overall in the NHL in 1993–94 (112 points).

Then came 1994 and playoff glory. There was the Cup-winning 3–2 victory over the stubborn Vancouver Canucks and the end of that cursed Curse, followed by the mammoth parade along lower Broadway's Canyon of Heroes. Coach Keenan even found time to bring the Cup to the annual Canadian Society's Hockey Dinner at the Waldorf where we all came forward to gawk at the Cup and put a thousand fingerprints all over it. He was some kind of hero that night.

Then he was gone — amidst allegations he'd been negotiating with Detroit for some time. But he wound up — not in Motor City, but underneath the Arch — in St. Louis. Gone for millions of dollars and the titles head coach and general manager. He proved once more there's no end to the twists and surprises and controversy in Mike Keenan's career.

Keenan guided St. Louis to their third-best regular season record in team history in the abbreviated (strike) season. But

Brett Hull and Keenan were soon going at each other like bulls batting heads. Then Keenan made some bad deals, discarding favorites like Brendan Shanahan and Curtis Joseph and acquiring shopworn players like Dale Hawerchuk and Joe Murphy. The fans fled the mammoth Keil Center as if they'd heard a bomb go off.

On December 19, 1996, Keenan, the sixth winningest coach in NHL history, was fired once again. He was left with the fascinating task of settling with the Blues on a four-year-plus pact calling for a reported $8–9 million to occupy his time.

His has been a stormy career and it's not over yet. Every astute hockey person predicts that Iron Mike, with expansion — even without it — will be back. New Yorkers don't care where he lands or when. They do remember what he did for them, how he helped bring them a Cup in '94. And how blissful it was!

Leetch, First American MVP

WHILE the Rangers were desperately clinging to a 3–2 lead over the Vancouver Canucks in the final seconds of the deciding game of the 1994 Stanley Cup finals, the votes were being tabulated for the MVP award — the Conn Smythe Trophy.

There was no doubt about the outcome. Defenseman Brian Leetch was the overwhelming choice — the first American and the first Ranger to have his name on the trophy since its inception in 1965.

Leetch led all playoff scorers with 34 points. His 11 goals and 23 assists were just three shy of Paul Coffey's playoff record for defensemen (37 points) in 1985. After the victory, the native of Corpus Christi, Texas, conversed with U.S. President Bill Clinton. He also appeared on the *Late Show* with David Letterman, the

Today Show, the *Howard Stern Show,* and *Late Night with Conan O'Brien.*

Then, along with Mark Messier and Nick Kypreos, he took the Stanley Cup to Yankee Stadium where the three Rangers took batting practice. The Yanks should have asked Leetch to throw a few. In high school, his fastball was timed at 90 miles per hour.

The Sweetest Victory

IT was a long wait — over half a century — but it finally happened. On June 14, 1994, the New York Rangers were crowned champions of hockey and skated off with the Stanley Cup. Swept aside were the curses, the jinxes, the bad luck, all the close calls and disappointments. In their place were joy and exultation, frolicking in the stands, on the ice, and in the streets. It was a celebration like no other in the city's hockey history.

The 1994 finals against the Vancouver Canucks ended in nail-biting fashion — a 3–2 Ranger victory in game seven, a game in which captain Mark Messier whacked in the winning goal.

"I've won the Stanley Cup six times," said Messier, "but this one was different. With all the history and bad luck this organization has had, it was the biggest challenge in pro sport to try to win here after 54 years."

In a previous series, one that went the limit against New Jersey, Messier had made a bold and startling prediction before game six. He declared the Rangers would defeat the Devils to force a seventh game in the Eastern Conference finals. Then he went out and scored a natural hat trick and added an assist in a memorable individual playoff performance. The Rangers won the game and then captured game seven back on home ice in dramatic style, with Stephane Matteau scoring the winner in double overtime.

Messier credited coach Mike Keenan's pregame pep talk for the 3–2 victory over the Canucks in the deciding game of the final series.

"He talked to us for about 15 minutes," said the captain. "It was the most intense, most emotional speech I've ever heard. He seized the moment. He took control of the situation. He came through when we needed him most."

"People don't know how difficult it is to win the Cup anywhere," said Keenan, who had lost in three previous attempts with Chicago and Philadelphia. "To win the Cup in New York took every bit of energy we had."

With the Cup victory imminent, outside the Garden, police braced themselves for what one grim-faced officer called "mob hysteria." "We're prepared for a riot," he said. But there was no riot in New York, only in Vancouver. Just thousands of fans enjoying the moment, with strangers hugging strangers and shouting themselves hoarse. One creative chap was seen hauling a garbage can around, decorated in silver paper, but a poor imitation of the Stanley Cup.

The magical season for the Rangers began with a two-game exhibition series in England against the Toronto Maple Leafs. Then the club roared through the regular season, compiling a 52-24-8 mark, the best in hockey. After winning the President's Trophy for finishing first overall, they survived seven-game struggles in the Eastern Conference final and in the Cup final to snare the 37-inch chunk of silverware that began as a small silver bowl in 1893, purchased by Canada's Governor General Lord Stanley for the princely sum of 50 dollars. That noble gentleman, who was recalled to England before the first Cup game was played, never envisioned his gift to hockey being paraded through the streets of New York after millions upon millions of dollars were spent in its capture.

With their triumph, the Rangers gladly handed over the mantle of the NHL's longest losers to the Detroit Red Wings, who had last tasted champagne from the Cup in 1955. (The Red Wings ended their own drought in 1997. The mantle now belongs to the Chicago Blackhawks, Stanley Cup winners in 1961.)

Rewarding the Winners

DURING the summer of 1994, the Rangers and their fans looked forward to the new season and especially to Monday, October 3, 1994 — Banner Night at Madison Square Garden. The new Stanley Cup banner would be hung from the rafters, alongside the championship banners from 1928, 1933, and 1940. The players also anticipated receiving their championship rings at a preseason dinner sometime before that date.

But a bitter summer-long dispute between the NHL Players' Association and the owners over a new collective bargaining agreement was unresolved in September. As a result, the players were locked out and the first few games of the new season were cancelled. Talks dragged on into October and November and more games were lost, including the All-Star game, scheduled for San Jose, January 21, 1995. It wasn't until January 11, 1995, that the NHL and the Players' Association came to an agreement and the rest of the season was saved.

If the Ranger players harbored any bitter feelings towards management over the lockout, they were quickly forgotten at a mid-January team function at the St. Regis Hotel. General manager Neil Smith presented each player with a stunning memento of the Cup victory — a 10-karat diamond-studded gold ring. Smith arranged for two dozen waiters to enter the dining room carrying the rings (enclosed in carved wooden boxes) on silver trays.

There were gasps from the players, their wives, and girlfriends when the boxes were opened. The rings were incredibly beautiful. They would remind each player for the rest of his life that he had played a role in achieving hockey's ultimate goal — the Stanley Cup.

It is not known when the tradition of presenting rings to Cup winners was first introduced, but it goes back to early in the century and possibly before. Big Billy Nicholson, a 300-pound goalie for Montreal, willed a Stanley Cup ring to his daughter — Helen Nicholson Woltho of Cornwall, Ontario — one of his rewards for leading his team to the Stanley Cup in 1902.

On the same night the Rangers received their rings, the Stanley Cup — fresh from the engravers — was on display. The players — for the first time — saw their names engraved on hockey's most famous trophy. There were 44 names in all, but two names were missing — Ed Olczyk and Mike Hartman. Both men had lumps in their throats. Neither had played in the 40 games required to qualify for the official list. The NHL had become diligent in keeping unworthy names off the Cup since Edmonton owner Peter Pocklington had managed to have his father's name inscribed on the trophy after one of the Oilers' triumphs in the '80s.

Despite the league's quota on names, Neil Smith and ex-Ranger Mike Gartner thought the exclusion of Olczyk and Hartman was unfair. Olczyk had played in 37 games (injuries kept him out of several more) and Hartman had dressed for 35.

At the time, Gartner was president of the NHL Players' Association. When a new collective bargaining agreement was agreed on and the lockout lifted, Gartner took NHL Commissioner Gary Bettman aside and pleaded with him to "bend the rules" and allow the names Olczyk and Hartman to be added to the Cup. Smith made a similar request. Bettman said he'd think about it.

Bettman's decision in favor of Olczyk and Hartman was announced at the dinner at the St. Regis. Cheers filled the room when it was announced the Stanley Cup would go back to the engravers — in order for those two more names to be added.

Big Bucks on Broadway

I N 1996–97, the New York Rangers were the big spenders in the NHL. General manager Neil Smith's player payroll amounted to $37.9 million, the highest expenditure on talent in NHL history. There were no fewer than nine million-dollar-a-year men on the Rangers, with Mark Messier on top ($6 million) and Wayne Gretzky next ($5,047,500). Neither Ranger came close to Mario Lemieux's salary of $11,321,429. The Penguins were second to the Rangers in spending, with a payroll of $34,314,682.

The Islanders had the lowest payroll at $13.7 million, while the Devils were tenth on the list with salaries totaling $23.4 million.

Despite the Rangers' free spending, veteran forward Pat Flatley was listed as the lowest-paid NHL player — at $125,000. However, Flatley earned a bonus of $100,000 when he played in his 40th game. He would have earned another $100,000 if he'd played in 80 games. Unfortunately, he appeared in only 67.

The Great One Still Has Goals to Achieve

W HEN the Rangers published their 1996–97 media guide, eight pages were reserved for the exploits of their newest star — Wayne Gretzky. The longer he plays, the more pages it will take to list his accomplishments.

Some of his goals couldn't be listed. One was to prove in his first season as a Ranger that he could still play the game. It disturbed him to hear talk, after a miserable season in St. Louis, that he'd lost a step and was skidding downhill fast. "It was a horrible time for me there," he says, "whereas playing in New York has been wonderful."

"The biggest difference," Wayne told Bob McKenzie of the *Hockey News*, "is having Mark (Messier) here, on and off the ice. On the ice, he opens up so much room for me. I'm not seeing the top checking line from the other team because Mark's line is. Off the ice, he takes away so much of the pressure. If we lose, it's not everyone crowding around asking me why. It was Mark's team before I got here and it's still Mark's team. I'm feeding off that energy."

Prior to the season, Wayne set some personal on-ice goals for himself. An easy one came early in the season, surpassing 1,800 assists. Next came 1,851 assists, an important milestone because it gave him as many career assists as Gordie Howe, his boyhood idol, had points. Another milestone he almost reached last season (he needed 76 assists and finished with 72) would have given him a truly unique sports record — more career assists than any other player has points. That astonishing accomplishment (something no hockey follower would have thought possible a few years ago) will be achieved early in the new season. Naturally, over the longer term, he's taking aim at 900 career goals. By season's end, he'd scored 862. Two more 20-goal seasons and that plateau will be surpassed.

And if he wants to become hockey's only 3,000-point man, he'd better plan on staying active for a few more years. He needs almost 300 more to achieve that lofty goal. Too bad he won't have Mark Messier in a Ranger uniform to help him. Here's to you, Wayne:

I've seen them all, boys
Seen the best
All the top snipers
from East to West
The Rocket, the Flower,
The Golden Jet,
Orr and Howe
Great scorers? You bet
But when all comparisons
Are over and done
It's Gretzky — the Great One
Who's still number one.

Rangers Rewarded
for Excellence

THE Ranger list of trophy winners is an impressive one, beginning with Bill Cook's capture of the Art Ross Trophy in 1927 and Frank Boucher's run of seven Lady Byng Trophies during the years 1928 to 1935. Here are the Rangers (winners and runners-up) who've won league honors for their skills on and off the ice.

Lady Byng Memorial Trophy
(sportsmanship and gentlemanly conduct)

> Frank Boucher — 1928 (7 wins from 1928 through 1935)
> Clint Smith — 1939
> Buddy O'Connor — 1948
> Edgar Laprade — 1950
> Andy Hebenton — 1957
> Camille Henry — 1958
> Jean Ratelle — 1972

— **Boucher** was runner-up to Joe Primeau in 1932.
— **Clint Smith** was runner-up to Gordie Drillon in 1938, Bobby Bauer in 1940.
— **Wally Hergesheimer** was runner-up to Red Kelly in 1953.
— **Don Raleigh** was runner-up to Red Kelly in 1954.
— **Danny Lewicki** was runner-up to Sid Smith in 1955.
— **Andy Hebenton** was runner-up to Alex Delvecchio in 1959 and to Don McKenney in 1960.
— **Camille Henry** was runner-up to Dave Keon in 1963.
— **Jean Ratelle** was runner-up to Gilbert Perreault in 1973.

James Norris Memorial Trophy
(best defenseman)

> Doug Harvey — 1962 (six more with Montreal)
> Harry Howell — 1967
> Brian Leetch — 1992, 1997

— **Bill Gadsby** was runner-up to Doug Harvey in 1956 and 1958 and to Tom Johnson in 1959.
— **Brad Park** was runner-up to Bobby Orr in 1970, 1971, 1972, 1974.

Hart Memorial Trophy
(most valuable player to his team)

> Ching Johnson — 1932 (over Howie Morenz)
> Buddy O'Connor — 1948 (over Frank Brimsek)
> Chuck Rayner — 1950 (over Ted Kennedy)
> Andy Bathgate — 1959 (over Gordie Howe)
> Mark Messier — 1992 (over Patrick Roy)

— **Bill Cook** was runner-up to Herb Gardiner in 1927 and to Eddie Shore in 1933.
— **Andy Bathgate** was runner-up to Gordie Howe in 1958.
— **Doug Harvey** was runner-up to Jacques Plante in 1962.
— **Ed Giacomin** was runner-up to Stan Mikita in 1967.

Vezina Trophy
(goaltender with lowest goals-against average)

> Dave Kerr — 1940
> Ed Giacomin, Gilles Villemure — 1971
> John Vanbiesbrouck — 1986

— **Dave Kerr** was runner-up to Norm Smith in 1937, to Tiny Thompson in 1938, and to Frank Brimsek in 1939.
— **Gump Worsley** and **Marcel Paille** were runners-up to Jacques Plante in 1958.

— **Ed Giacomin** was runner-up to Jacques Plante and Glenn Hall in 1969.
— **Ed Giacomin** and **Gilles Villemure** were runners-up to Ken Dryden in 1973.

Art Ross Trophy
(scoring leader)

Bill Cook — 1927 (1-point margin over Dick Irvin)
Bill Cook — 1933 (6-point margin over Harvey Jackson)
Bryan Hextall — 1942 (2-point margin over Lynn Patrick)

— **Hextall** and **Patrick** were among five players who tied for second place (18 points) behind Bill Cowley in 1941.
— **Buddy O'Connor** was runner-up by a single point to Elmer Lach in 1948.
— **Andy Bathgate** was runner-up to Bobby Hull in 1962. They tied in points with 84 but Hull scored 50 goals, Bathgate 28.
— **Bathgate** was runner-up (by five points) to Gordie Howe in 1963.

Calder Memorial Trophy
(top rookie)

Kilby MacDonald — 1940 (Wally Stanowski, Tor.)
Grant Warwick — 1942 (Buddy O'Connor, Mtl.)
Edgar Laprade — 1946 (George Gee, Chi.)
Pentti Lund — 1949 (Allan Stanley, NYR)
Lorne Worsley — 1953 (Gord Hannigan, Tor.)
Camille Henry — 1954 (Earl Reibel, Det.)
Steve Vickers — 1973 (Bill Barber, Pha.)
Brian Leetch — 1989 (Trevor Linden, Van.)

— **Bert Connolly** (13 goals in 87 NHL games) was runner-up to Dave Schriner in 1935.
— **Allan Stanley** was runner-up to teammate Pentti Lund in 1949.

— Hy Buller was runner-up to Bernie Geoffrion in 1952.
— Andy Hebenton was runner-up to Glenn Hall in 1956.
— Bill Fairbairn was runner-up to Tony Esposito in 1970.
— Don Murdoch was runner-up to Willi Plett in 1977.

Bill Masterton Memorial Trophy
(perseverance, sportsmanship, and dedication to hockey)

Jean Ratelle — 1971
Rod Gilbert — 1976
Anders Hedberg — 1985

Lester Patrick Trophy
(for outstanding service to hockey in the U.S.)

General John R. Kilpatrick — 1968
William Jennings, Terry Sawchuk — 1971
Murray Murdoch — 1974
Bill Chadwick, Ranger associate — 1975
Phil Esposito — 1978
Fred Shero — 1980
Emile Francis — 1982
Lynn Patrick — 1989
Rod Gilbert — 1991
Frank Boucher — 1993
Brian Mullen — 1995

Conn Smythe Trophy
(MVP of playoffs)

Brian Leetch — 1994

Lester B. Pearson Award
(outstanding player selected by members of NHLPA)

Jean Ratelle — 1972
Mark Messier — 1992 (also won in 1990 as an Oiler)

Jack Adams Award
(to NHL coach)

Since the award was introduced in 1974, no Ranger coach has been a winner. **Fred Shero** was runner-up in 1979, **Roger Neilson** in 1992.

Frank J. Selke Trophy
(best defensive forward)

Since the award was introduced in 1978, no Ranger has been a winner or a runner-up.

King Clancy Memorial Trophy
(leadership and humanitarian contributions to his community)

Adam Graves — 1994

William M. Jennings Trophy
(goaltender(s) with fewest goals against)

Since the award was introduced in 1982, no Ranger goalie has been a winner or a runner-up.

President's Trophy
(to the club with best regular-season record)

Winner receives $200,000 to be split evenly between the club and the players.

New York Rangers — 1992, 1994

In 1994, despite having no 100-point scorers and no players among the top 10 individual scorers, the Rangers finished with 52 victories and 112 points, five more wins and six more points than second-place New Jersey.

THE RANGERS
THROUGH THE YEARS

1926: ON MAY 15, 1926, the New York Rangers are granted an NHL franchise. The NHL becomes a 10-team league with a Canadian and an American Division.

1927: RANGERS FINISH ATOP the American Division with a 25-13-6 record in 44 games. Bill Cook is the NHL's leading scorer with 33 goals and four assists for 37 points. During the season, the Americans sue to restrain Madison Square Garden from allowing the temperature in the arena to rise above 40 degrees for hockey games. It is reduced to 55 degrees and no further.

1928: RANGERS WIN THEIR FIRST STANLEY CUP by defeating Montreal Maroons in the finals. Manager Lester Patrick takes over in goal for the injured Lorne Chabot in game two. Rangers win in overtime 2–1 and go on to capture the series three games to two. Rangers become only the second U.S. team to win the Cup.

1930: BEGINNING ON FEBRUARY 27, 1930, the Rangers play four consecutive tie games. For the first time in history, two American teams — the Bruins and the Rangers — meet in the Stanley Cup finals. The Bruins win the two-game series by scores of 2–0 and 2–1.

1932: RANGERS FINISH FIRST IN THEIR DIVISION, but lose 3–0 to Toronto in Stanley Cup finals. Bill Cook, with 34 goals, shares scoring lead with Toronto's Charlie Conacher. Leafs beat New York in Cup finals in three straight games — a playoff first.

1933: BILL COOK LEADS NHL SCORERS for second time with 50 points in 48 games. Rangers win their second Stanley Cup, defeating Toronto three games to one in finals.

1934: THE PENALTY-SHOT RULE is introduced and the Rangers miss on their first four attempts.

1936: BERT CONNOLLY FINALLY SCORES the first penalty-shot goal for the Rangers. Rangers miss the playoffs for the first time in franchise history.

1937: THE DETROIT RED WINGS DEFEAT the Rangers three games to two in the Stanley Cup finals. New York's Alex Shibicky takes the first penalty shot in finals history and is stopped by rookie netminder Earl Robertson.

1938: THE AMERICANS EDGE THE RANGERS 3–2 in the fourth overtime period of game three to win a playoff series. A description of the contest, witnessed by 16,340 fans, becomes the first hockey story to be featured on the front page of the *New York Times*.

1939: RANGER REJECT MEL HILL scores three overtime goals as the Bruins eliminate the Rangers in the playoffs. Lester Patrick turns the Ranger coaching job over to Frank Boucher.

1940: THE RANGERS DEFEAT the Toronto Maple Leafs four games to two to win the Stanley Cup. Lynn and Muzz Patrick become the third and fourth members of the Patrick family to have their names engraved on the Stanley Cup. New York's Kilby MacDonald, a 25-year-old rookie, wins the Calder Trophy.

1942: THE RANGERS ARE SURPRISE first-place finishers over Toronto. The two clubs meet in the first round of the play-offs, Toronto winning in six games. Bryan Hextall, with 56 points, finishes two points ahead of teammate Lynn Patrick in the scoring race. Grant Warwick, with 16 goals, wins the Calder Trophy as top rookie.

1943: THE RANGERS' PHIL WATSON is frozen in an essential war job in Montreal and is refused permission to play hockey in New York. Watson joins the Canadiens in return for Charlie Sands and Dutch Hiller. Rangers introduce a 17-year-old rookie — Don Raleigh. Another rookie, Lloyd Mohns, plays an afternoon game with the New York Rovers, has a postgame date with skating legend Sonja Henie, and is called back to play for the Rangers that evening.

1944: RANGERS WIN ONLY SIX GAMES in the 1943–44 season. Frank Boucher, 42, makes a comeback and collects 14 points in 15 games. Bryan Hextall claims exemption from war service as a farmer and is barred from entering the United States. He sits out a year. Rangers lose by 15–0 to Detroit in league's most lopsided game.

1945: RANGER COACH INTRODUCES the two-goalie system and rotates Charlie Rayner with Sugar Jim Henry.

1946: THE LAST-PLACE RANGERS (13-28-9) average 14,400 fans for the 1945–46 season. Edgar Laprade wins the Calder Trophy (15 goals) as a 26-year-old rookie. Rangers make first change in uniform design, adding numerals to the front of the jerseys and Rangers spelled out above the numerals in the shape of a half-moon.

1947: ON JANUARY 2, 1947, goalie Charlie Rayner became a sixth attacker for New York against Toronto at Maple Leaf Gardens. With 35 seconds left to play and his team trailing by a goal, Rayner skated up to the Toronto blueline, hoping to score. Leafs won 5–4. Lester Patrick Night is held at Madison Square Garden.

1948: FRANK BOUCHER RELINQUISHES his job as Rangers' coach and is replaced by Lynn Patrick. Four Rangers — Buddy O'Connor, Frank Eddolls, Bill Moe, and Edgar Laprade are injured in an auto accident, and another on-ice injury suffered by Don Raleigh results in a last-place finish.

1949: PENTTI LUND, the Rangers' first Finnish-born player, captures the Calder Trophy after a 14–goal season.

1950: THE DETROIT RED WINGS DEFEAT the Rangers four games to three in the Stanley Cup finals. When the circus forces the Rangers out of Madison Square Garden, the team plays two playoff games in Toronto, the other five in Detroit. The Rangers' Don Raleigh ties a playoff record with his second over-time goal in as many games. Rangers do not win another playoff series for 21 years.

1951: ON DECEMBER 6, BILL COOK takes over the coaching reins from Neil Colville. The Rangers bring up Vic Howe, Gordie's brother. Howe scores a goal in a three-game trial.

1952: CHICAGO'S BILL MOSIENKO scores a record three goals in 21 seconds against the Rangers and rookie goaltender Lorne Anderson. Only 3,250 fans witness the history-making event.

1953: CALDER TROPHY WINNER Gump Worsley is replaced by Johnny Bower, who plays in all 70 games. Bill Cook ends his coaching career.

1954: DOUG BENTLEY COMES out of retirement to join the Rangers. Bentley produces four points in his first game (an 8–3 rout of Boston). Camille Henry (24 goals) wins the Calder Trophy.

1955: GENERAL MANAGER FRANK BOUCHER is replaced by Muzz Patrick, who hires Phil Watson to coach the Rangers.

1956: RANGERS FINISH REGULAR SEASON OVER .500 (32-28-10) for the first time since 1941–42. They lose to Montreal (45-15-10) in the playoffs.

1959: RANGERS BLOW A NINE-POINT LEAD with two weeks left in the season, allowing the Leafs to steal fourth place and a playoff berth. Early in the 1959–60 season, Alf Pike replaces Phil Watson as Ranger coach.

1961: DOUG HARVEY, 36, is signed as playing coach of the 1961–62 Rangers and becomes the first Ranger to win the Norris Trophy.

1962: RED SULLIVAN IS NAMED RANGER COACH on December 28, 1962.

1963: ANDY BATHGATE sets a "modern-day" league record by scoring in 10 consecutive games.

1965: RANGERS CALL UP FORWARD ULF STERNER, the first European-born and -trained player to sign with an NHL club. Sterner plays in four games, collects no points, and is returned to the minors. Emile Francis fires coach Red Sullivan and assumes dual role as general manager and coach.

1966: ON MARCH 12, CHICAGO'S Bobby Hull scores his record-breaking 51st goal of the season against the Rangers and goaltender Cesare Maniago at the Chicago Stadium. The Rangers coax "Boom Boom" Geoffrion out of retirement and his spark helps put the Rangers into the playoffs for the first time since 1962.

1967: DEFENSEMAN HARRY HOWELL becomes the first Ranger to play in over 1,000 games and is honored on Harry Howell Night.

1968: THE RANGERS OPEN THE NEW Madison Square Garden in February with a 3–1 victory over the Flyers. Rangers sign Boom Boom Geoffrion as coach. Philadelphia and Oakland play a neutral-site game at the Garden on March 3, 1968, after the roof blows off the Philadelphia Spectrum. Fans are admitted free.

1969: MANAGER EMILE FRANCIS SIGNS himself to a $1 contract when a blizzard sweeps through New York and Eddie Giacomin is a no-show. But backup Don Simmons arrives in time to play and 43-year-old Francis serves as the Ranger backup.

1970: RANGER GOALTENDER TERRY SAWCHUK dies in hospital after a fight with roommate Ron Stewart. A police investigation clears Stewart.

1971: VIC HADFIELD TOSSES TORONTO goalie Bernie Parent's face mask into the crowd during a playoff game and it disappears. Rangers set 15 club records during regular season.

1972: LEFT WING VIC HADFIELD scores twice in final game of season and becomes the first Ranger to hit the 50-goal plateau. But the Bruins win the Cup on New York ice in the final series.

1973: LARRY POPEIN has brief run as Ranger coach.

1975: THE ISLANDERS' J.P. PARISE ends the Ranger season with a stunning goal after 11 seconds of overtime in the first all–New York playoff series. Ron Stewart takes over as coach. On November 2, 1975, Ed Giacomin is placed on waivers and claimed by Detroit.

1976: RANGERS CELEBRATE THEIR 50th season in the NHL. On January 7, 1976, John Ferguson takes over as Ranger coach and general manager, replacing Emile Francis and Ron Stewart. Rangers trade Rick Middleton to Boston for Ken Hodge.

1977: RANGER FANS HONOR ROD GILBERT with special night. Jean Guy Talbot is hired as coach.

1978: ON JUNE 2, GENERAL MANAGER John Ferguson and coach Jean Guy Talbot are fired. Fred Shero is signed as general manager and coach.

1979: ISLANDER DEFENSEMAN DENIS POTVIN checks Ulf Nilsson into boards, snapping the Ranger star's ankle. Nilsson never fully recovers and the incident prompts everlasting "Potvin sucks" chant.

1980: RANGERS SELECT CENTER JIM MALONE with their number one draft pick. Malone never plays a game in the NHL. On November 19, Fred Shero is replaced by Craig Patrick.

1981: CRAIG PATRICK HIRES HERB BROOKS as Ranger coach. Rangers respond with 92-point season.

1982: ON APRIL 8, 1982, MIKKO LEINONEN of the Rangers becomes the first player to record six assists in a playoff game, helping his club to a 7–3 win over Philadelphia in game two of their Patrick Division final. Leinonen's mark is equaled by Edmonton's Wayne Gretzky in 1987.

1985: IN JANUARY 1985, HERB BROOKS is relieved as coach and replaced by Craig Patrick. On April 13, Philadelphia Flyers' Tim Kerr sets a new playoff mark by scoring four goals in one period against the Rangers. In the off-season, Ted Sator is signed as the new Ranger coach.

1986: PHIL ESPOSITO REPLACES CRAIG PATRICK as Ranger general manager. Rangers draft a junior defenseman named Joe Ranger. Esposito fires Ted Sator and replaces him with Tom Webster. Webster's health problems force Esposito to handle both jobs.

1987: ESPOSITO SURRENDERS a number one draft pick to sign coach Michel Bergeron of Quebec.

1989: NEIL SMITH IS HIRED as general manager. Smith signs Roger Neilson as new Ranger coach. Brian Leetch wins Calder Trophy. Esposito fires Michel Bergeron on the eve of the 1989 playoffs and takes over as coach. Rangers are swept in four straight games by Pittsburgh in playoffs. Esposito is let go as coach and general manager.

1990: JOURNEYMAN JOHN DRUCE FIRES nine goals in five games for Washington, including the overtime series winner, as the Caps vanquish the Rangers in a playoff series.

1991: RANGERS ACQUIRE Mark Messier and Adam Graves as free agents.

1992: RANGERS FINISH ATOP the overall standings for the first time in 50 years. Then lose playoff series to Pittsburgh after beating Devils.

1993: RON SMITH REPLACES ROGER NEILSON as coach in January 1993. Rangers miss playoffs and Neil Smith signs Mike Keenan as new coach.

1994: THE RANGERS POST two consecutive 6–0 shutouts over the New York Islanders to open the Stanley Cup playoffs. They are the first back-to-back shutouts to open the playoffs since Buffalo blanked Montreal 1–0 and 3–0 in 1983. Rangers eliminate Isles, Capitals, Devils, and Canucks to capture their first Stanley Cup in 54 years. Within a month, Mike Keenan leaves New York for St. Louis. Colin Campbell is named the new head coach.

1995: RAISING OF THE STANLEY CUP BANNER is postponed until January 20 because of a shortened 48-game season. Rangers are eliminated in second playoff round by Philadelphia.

1996: ON JULY 20, 1996, WAYNE GRETZKY, 35, signs a two-year contract with New York that reunites him with former teammate Mark Messier.